CRUCIAL GUITAR BASICS

GUITAR 101:
BUYING THE RIGHT GUITAR AND GEAR,
LEARNING CHORDS AND SCALES
(NO THEORY REQUIRED!).
FOR BEGINNERS AND BEYOND.

Steve Cabain

Please Review This Book!

If you enjoy this book and get value from it, please leave a review on Amazon, as that would really help me and hopefully future readers too. Even critical points help me to refine the book even further and I read and am grateful for every review I receive.

The QR code below will take you straight to the review page.

Many Thanks! Steve

Contents

Just for You!

If you'd like to receive a free audiobook version of this book, then use the email below and this will be sent to your inbox as soon as it's published.

stevecabain@gmail.com

Please state AUDIOBOOK in the subject title of your email and provide your first name.

Please allow at least 2 days for me to respond to your request.

Introduction

The guitar has a kind of grit and excitement
possessed by nothing else.

Brian May

After months of playing air guitar to 'Free Bird", what really got me into guitar was watching a documentary about Jimi Hendrix and picking up the Woodstock soundtrack. Listening to his version of 'Star Spangled Banner' and 'Purple Haze.' My brother played acoustic guitar and, idolising him, I thought,

'I'm going to get a guitar'.

Kirk Hammett

OK, you've decided to learn to play the guitar.

This is a great decision, in my opinion.

The guitar is a versatile instrument that can play a wide variety of music. It also has the merit of being very affordable from entry-level acoustic guitars at £35 ($50). Whilst at the other end of the spectrum, you can pay many thousands for a custom shop model and even many hundreds of thousands at auction for guitars played by famous players (one day that could be your Axe for sale!).

Given you're taking an interest in this book my assumption is that you are new to guitar and are looking for information advice and guidance on the features of guitars and what to consider when it comes to buying, owning and playing them. This book is aimed at you! This will hopefully cover all the questions you have, including some you didn't even know you had, but didn't have anyone to ask them to. Let me be your guide.

So why put your trust in me, well I've been there where you are right now, and I've been owning and more importantly playing guitars for well over 40 years. I've been in numerous bands and even done some recording sessions. I've therefore accumulated a lot of knowledge along the way, but even I'm still learning my craft, and indeed there have even been a few things that I've learnt in writing this book. This book is therefore aimed at fast forwarding you on your journey by imparting things that are very useful to know if you're learning guitar.

How did I start out? Well, aged ten on a Folk nylon string guitar and indeed playing Folk music at school. This taught me open chords and the Blues Pentatonic scale!

I couldn't wait to get my first electric, though, and this happened on my 13th birthday - a day that is etched in my memory as a result. The amplifier had to wait a while, however, and the only way I could initially get sound out of my Les Paul-copy (which I still have for sentimental reasons) was by butting it up against a large wardrobe in my bedroom to act as a sound hole! Such was my determination, and I'm glad that I stuck with it, because it has given me a great deal of enjoyment and indeed a sense of achievement.

What you will learn in this book.

- A brief whizz through the anatomy of the guitar (when people start talking about fixed or floating bridges, for example, you will be able to nod in a sagely fashion).

- How many strings should it have?

- Acoustic v Electric – the key differences that you need to understand when you're starting out on your guitar playing journey.

- Budgets – what can you expect to pay.

- Where to shop and why.

- Amps and other accessories.   Including tone secrets.

- Options for learning guitar.

- Chords and scales to learn.

- Who's worth listening to for inspiration?

For complete clarity, this book is aimed at bringing you up to speed on issues to do with the guitar. It is not a book on how to play the guitar, as such. There are many of these on the market for you to choose from when you're ready for that stage. I will, however, give you a head start with basic chords to learn and how to read chord charts and TAB (guitar music – it's extremely easy to understand, in fact, I'm told even drummers can understand it). What I will say though is be very cautious of those books that state you'll be playing in 7 days - you might be after a fashion; it really depends on what your definition of playing is!

I say this because playing the guitar is a motor skill, just like sports, and the reality is that it takes practice, a lot of it, if you plan on becoming moderately proficient, which is **absolutely** attainable by the way. Learning the guitar is not something you can do overnight though; it does take time and practice, but ultimately knowing that you've put in the effort to get to the level you achieve does feel great.

Why bother then? Well playing the guitar is a great deal of fun whether you're learning your favourite songs at home or in a garage or rehearsal studio with your mates. Or potentially even entertaining an audience.

There are, however, a great many guitars to choose from, and indeed amps for that matter, and this can make the task feel overwhelming. This might make you anxious about making the wrong choice. Added to this that there is a whole new language connected to guitars to learn about, and this can make it seem rather confusing and complicated. It doesn't have to be, because as I will show you once you get a handle on the terminology and go out and look and play some guitars (more on this later), then you will see that I've demystified the process! You don't want to be baffled by a salesman when you come to make your key buying decision as you could walk out with a poor-quality guitar, possibly from a big brand that isn't really what you want and just doesn't feel right. This would be a bad way to begin your guitar playing adventure.

So, before we dive into the nitty-gritty have a think about what it is that is driving you towards the guitar. Is there a certain style of music or even a specific band that motivates you? Is Folk your thing or Heavy Metal? Are you captivated by Country or rocked by Rock! You may even want to play all types of music. The answer to these questions will be a key influencing factor in your choice of guitar and indeed amp, should you want to go down the electric route.

Another factor will naturally be your budget.

Are you flush having saved up a decent wad? Or is someone else planning on buying the guitar for you (if so – sweet!).

As I've said, entry-level guitars are extremely affordable, but within reason, you do tend to get what you pay for. The guitar itself might essentially be a glorified plank of wood with strings attached, but what the wood is and what is attached to it does make a big difference to the sound produced and at the end of the day you play the guitar to make sounds that will hopefully sound great.

Now we come to the potentially awkward bit when choosing a guitar – you want to hear it. This is typically done by playing it, but if this is your first guitar that might not be possible, because you haven't yet had a guitar to learn on. There are ways around this, but a key element of the decision-making process could be out of your hands, which is not ideal. If you have not already done so, it would therefore be worth asking a guitar-playing friend to show you how to play a few chords before you rush out with your hard-earned cash to make a purchase. This will let you see what playing the guitar entails, and this will hopefully reinforce your desire to learn the instrument. Alternatively, as I've said already, it could show you that the process of learning guitar in the early days involves considerable effort and repetition. If this isn't for you after all, then I've just saved you time and money!

Let's assume however you have done the above exercise and are still 'lovin' it' and you want to learn to be the next Ed Sheeran, Eric Clapton or Kirk Hammett. See what BB King had to say on the topic of learning.

The beautiful thing about learning is that nobody can take it away from you.

BB King

In this book we'll cover what you'll want to have with your guitar e.g. an amp and effects and where to go for lessons and round it all off with some ideas around players to listen to. When you wrap it all up, you're going to be very well equipped to make the most out of your guitar playing journey.

Let's dive right in - here are the things I think you should know right away.

1

The Fundamentals

I'm only myself when I have a guitar in my hands.

George Harrison

A BRIEF WHIZ THROUGH THE ANATOMY OF THE GUITAR

Skip this bit if this is old news, but so that we're all on the same page (if you'll excuse the pun) it's worth setting this out for the record.

Starting from the top, the 'standard' guitar consists of:

The Head (well usually - there are a few guitars that don't include heads)

The Neck

The Body

To the Head are attached Machine Heads or Tuners. These allow you to change the pitch of the strings and keep the guitar in tune. Depending on the shape of the Head, there will usually be either 6 tuners in a line or 3 either side. On guitars with 6 tuners in a line on the Head, you may also have a small device attached to it called a String Tree. This holds down the top E and B strings in order to keep the angle over the Nut similar to the other strings. Occasionally you might see a second string tree used to hold down the G and D strings as well. As for the tuners, these are basically winding mechanisms that tighten or loosen the strings. They come in two primary varieties, either standard tuners or locking tuners. Entry-level instruments are unlikely to have locking tuners as these are more expensive to produce. Locking tuners make changing strings slightly easier and are considered to offer better tuning stability, but this might largely be because they are typically well-made units and it isn't necessarily a function of their design as such.

At the top of the Neck is a thin strip of material called the Nut. This can be plastic or graphite or a similar substance, in some cases, it is made from bone (I couldn't tell you from which animal, because I don't know). The Nut has grooves cut into it. These keep the strings in place and at a set distance from one another. Despite this being a small element of the guitar, it can influence the tone and sustain of the instrument a fair bit. The good news is that a good quality replacement nut can be bought and fitted at relatively low cost and this is something for you to consider later on in your guitar playing career.

On the Neck sit metal strips of wire; these are the Frets. These stand out from the Neck and so when you press down on the string behind a fret with enough pressure the string touches the fret and reduces the effective length of the string. This makes the pitch higher. As the frets go up the fingerboard towards the body of the guitar, they get progressively closer together. This is to ensure that the pitch of the notes remains correct. The number of frets on the Neck varies, but is usually 21 on an electric guitar and 20 on an acoustic (however on an acoustic unless the body is cut away these will be extremely difficult to play passed the 12th fret!).

The Body is an element of the guitar that has a significant influence on the sound. It is typically made of wood. In an acoustic guitar, it is a fairly standard shape, with a hollow body and a sound hole of some description on the front face of the guitar. With electric guitars, however, the shape can vary considerably including the wild and outlandish such as the guitar played by Prince in later years. You will, however, find that most entry-level guitars conform to just a few classic guitar shapes, usually a Strat shape with a double-cutaway or a Les Paul shape with a single-cutaway at the bottom.

Then on the body at the other end of the strings, we find the Bridge and the Saddles. These secure the strings to the body. In broad terms, the bridge will either be fixed or will move, pivoting on an edge, so that the strings can be bent sharp or flat.

For the Electric guitar, there are other elements that need to be included in order to get the guitar to sound loud (sometimes extremely loud!!!). These start with the Pickups. They take the vibration of the strings and take it to the output on the guitar (this is the jack into which the cable between the guitar and the amp goes). There are typically a few controls on the top of the guitar that cover Volume and Tone and a switch that allows you to select which pickups are on, assuming you have more than one.

So largely speaking that covers the basics of what the guitar is, but there is one key consideration related to this that needs to be considered – are you left or right-handed?

LEFT OR RIGHT-HANDED?

If you're right-handed, you'll play the guitar by strumming or picking with your right hand and playing chords and notes with your left. It might sound odd that you use your dominant hand for what sounds like the easy bit, but that is typically how it is. As you know most people are right-handed and therefore the selection of right-handed instruments is far greater than left-handed ones. As a result of this is that if you are left-handed is relatively easy to address with an acoustic, as the strings on a right-handed guitar can be switched around (not ideal though as the Nut and the saddle of the bridge might be set up for a right-handed player) it's a bit more involved with an electric guitar. You could learn to play a right-handed guitar or settle for the more limited choice (there could still be a good one available for you) or have one custom-made if you have the budget (I wouldn't recommend this at this stage).

Did you know that Jimi Hendrix played right handed guitars and re-strung them, because he thought they were better quality than the left-handed models available at that time? It was a factor in his sound, as it altered the angle of the bridge pickup on the Strats he usually played, as well as the position of the tremolo.

HOW MANY STRINGS SHOULD IT HAVE?

Most guitars have 6 strings.

These are tuned low to high as follows E-A-D-G-B-e (this is referred to as standard tuning, I'll cover other common tunings later in this book).

You can remember this order by learning the phrase:

Eddie Ate Dynamite Good-Bye Eddie

(Thanks to Mike from The-Art-of-Guitar, for this useful tip).

The top E (usually denoted using a lower-case e) is actually the one at the bottom of the guitar. Still, as it's the thinnest string it has the highest note, hence it's referred to as the top E. Sometimes numbers are used when referring to the strings, in which case the 6th string is the Low E and so on as follows: 6th (E), 5th (A), 4th (D), 3rd (G), 2nd (B) and 1st (e).

More recently lower thicker strings have been added to some guitars and are popular in Heavy Metal for example. There are therefore also 7 string guitars and sometimes even 8 string ones. The most common tuning for a 7 string guitar is

13

(low to high) B-E-A-D-G-B-e, and for an 8 string it's usually the same, but with the lowest string tuned to F#. Some players, however, prefer to tune the lowest string down a whole step to A on a 7 string or to E on an 8 string.

More commonly, there are 12 string guitars,. These have thin strings running next to the standard strings, i.e. the E-A-D-G-B-e. These guitars are essentially played in the same way as a bulk standard 6 string. Still, the additional strings do impart a different sound (listen to the open bars of Hotel California or the first electric guitar element of Stairway to Heaven for examples). For those starting out 6 strings is the way to go in my opinion. You can always add more guitars with more strings, later, should you wish to do so.

2

Acoustic or Electric?

Let me explain something about guitar playing. Everyone's got their own character, and that's the thing that's amazed me about guitar playing since the first day I picked it up. Everyone's approach to what can come out of six strings is different from another person, but it's all valid.

Jimmy Page

ACOUSTIC OR ELECTRIC?

There is a school of thought that says that learning on an acoustic makes you a better player in the long term. I'm looking at this through the prism of over 40 years and learning on an acoustic (Classical style) myself for the first few years, so I feel I'm biased, it worked out OK for me. There is however a school of thought that says if someone wants an electric guitar and is given or gets an acoustic this can be a real turn-off, plus electrics can be easier to play, so these are arguments for getting an electric straight away.

If you're going to learn to play lead guitar, get an electric guitar ... it doesn't have to be an expensive one ... acoustic guitars aren't good for learning lead, because you can't play up very high on the neck and they take heavier-gauge strings, which makes it hard to bend notes.

Eddie Van Halen

Certainly, I couldn't wait to get my first electric, which as I've said happened on my 13th birthday. The amplifier had to wait a bit though, and Eddie was right it's much easier to play lead guitar on an electric.

Let's consider the most important differences between them.

TYPE	ACOUSTIC GUITAR	ELECTRIC GUITAR
Body	**Hollow body.** When plucked the strings vibrate the entire guitar. The sound is passed into the body of the guitar, where it is naturally amplified.	**Solid body (usually).** This requires electric amplification to produce sound.
Size and weight	**Larger** than electric guitars, because the body has to amplify the sound. However, they're usually light weight given they're mainly hollow.	**Generally smaller**, but much heavier than acoustic guitars. The weight is very influenced by the wood used in the body and the thickness of the body itself.
Neck	**Usually a bit thicker** than on electric guitars and the strings are further apart. Classical guitars have even wider necks.	**Typically, slightly thinner** than on acoustic guitars. The strings are also closer together as a result.
Strings	Can either be made of **nylon** (classical or Spanish style guitars) or **steel** (folk style guitars). The steel variety tends to be heavier gauge (thickness) than on electrics, as they need to vibrate more strongly to produce the sound. This	Use thinner, lighter **steel** strings, which can be easier on the fingers. Strings on electric guitars don't need to be heavy-gauge, because the sound is amplified. The thinner strings make playing lead guitar

		in turn makes them harder to hold down, so lead guitar techniques are harder to achieve on steel-strung acoustic guitars. Nylon strings are lighter than the steel variety, which makes them easier to play, but they have a more subtle tone and tend to be slightly quieter.	techniques, such as vibratos and bends easier.
String action		Acoustic guitars typically have heavier gauge strings to increase the volume, and these need more room to vibrate, so they need to be a bit **further away from the Neck**. This is another factor that can make acoustic guitars harder to play. Guitars with nylon strings however are not much harder to play and if anything are probably just as easy as electric guitars.	Since the strings on electric guitars tend to be thinner than on acoustics, they don't need that much space to resonate. **The string action can be set lower as a result**. As the strings are closer to the Neck, this makes them easier to fret.
Tone		Acoustic guitars without amplification **have a single tone**. There are however tonal differences between different acoustic guitars, and this is the result of	It's possible to get different sounds out of electric guitars because they usually have several pickups and tone controls. In addition, the

	materials used in the manufacture of the guitar and the size of the instrument, which can affect both the tone and volume of the guitar.	characteristics of the amp being used and any effects that are added can give you a **wide variety of tonal possibilities** – even using the guitar to sound like a different instrument if you really want it to!
Musical application	The lack of amplification tends to **limit the use of acoustic guitars to music where a clean acoustic tone sounds good**. These include Country, Classical, Traditional Blues, Pop and Folk.	Since electric guitars are amplified, and effects can be added to create a final tone, you can **more or less play any type of music** with them (arguably other than Classical and Folk).

THE ACOUSTIC GUITAR - PROS AND CONS

PROS OF LEARNING ON AN ACOUSTIC GUITAR

- If you can play something on a steel-string acoustic guitar, you should also be able to play it easily on an electric. The same can not necessarily be said moving from playing something on an electric to playing it on an acoustic.

- Many people (your household, neighbours etc.) will prefer the naturally soothing, calmer tone of the acoustic over the possibly distorted, and probably loud, tone of an amplified electric.

- Acoustic guitars are light and easy to transport. Great for taking round to friend's houses or on camping trips for those 'round the campfire' singalongs!

- You don't need to buy cables or an amplifier to begin playing. The acoustic guitar is an all in one solution!

- They can be extremely inexpensive, so are a great option if money is tight (but I recommend the Spanish/Classical guitar variety initially).

CONS OF LEARNING ON AN ACOUSTIC GUITAR

- Steel strung acoustic guitars can be much tougher on your fingers than an electric. To put this into context, an absolute beginner will probably only be able to play for about 20 minutes before needing to take a break due to painful fingertips. This might be short term; however, as providing you are not put off and persevere, you should develop tougher fingertips after a few weeks.

- The harder strings also mean that playing chords will be much harder, especially barre chords, where you press down most or all of the strings with your first or pointing finger.

- There is the risk of more string buzz due to the effort required to fret harder strings. This is where the string is not pressed down enough, and a buzz is created between the string and the top of the fret being fretted. This is not a sound you want!

- Acoustic guitars tend to have wider fret boards, and this is something that beginners may find adds to the challenge of learning.

- Acoustic guitars tend to be less robust than electric guitars. It's not good to throw either of them around, but acoustic guitars would like the experience less!

THE ELECTRIC GUITAR - PROS AND CONS

PROS OF LEARNING ON AN ELECTRIC GUITAR

- The strings on electric guitars are usually lighter gauge than acoustic steel-string guitars, and this makes them easier on your fingers.

- Playing barre chords is also easier on the electric, because of the lightness of the strings.

- Holding down chords, in general, is easier on an electric than an acoustic because the neck will usually be narrower.

- You can often plug headphones into your amplifier, so you won't drive your neighbours crazy (be careful of the volume and level of distortion though, as this can be a recipe for hearing loss if done over a sustained period).

CONS OF LEARNING ON AN ELECTRIC GUITAR

- It's almost certainly going to cost more than the acoustic option, because you'll need to buy an amplifier and guitar lead as well.

- Finding the right tone is not always easy for beginners (but this is also part of the fun - providing you don't spend all your time focused on finding interesting sounds and remember to practice playing!).

- If you can play something on an electric that will not necessarily mean that you can play it on an acoustic guitar as well.

WHICH IS IT TO BE?

That's your call, but there is still more to learn about and consider. You should, of course, try both and let that inform your decision. Even if you know now with 100% certainty which one you want, it's still fun to try the other variety, for future reference if for no other reason. Plus, almost certainly, if you continue to learn guitar, you'll want to expand your guitar collection. This could be a means of broadening the style of music you play, and this will let you fill the gap and open up new tones and musical experiences.

As I said earlier in the introduction, you should give consideration to the type of music that you like. Buying a Classical style guitar and hoping to bash out Heavy Metal, for example, is likely to be doomed to failure! However, Zakk Wylde (Black Label Society) manages to do this very effectively (he does use an amplified acoustic though).

(See Zakk Wylde playing Voodoo Child on an electro-acoustic and even Black Sabbath on a 1962 Hello Kitty(!) guitar on YouTube).

3

What about the Wood?

*It all comes down to the density
of the wood.
Every guitar's different.*

Robin Trower

WHAT ABOUT THE WOOD? ACOUSTIC GUITARS

The type, quality and combination of woods used in the production of a guitar all contribute to its tone. Entry-level models tend to be made of laminated wood, which does not mature as it gets older, so what you hear is what you get! Intermediate guitars, however, generally feature solid wood tops combined with laminated back and sides. The best instruments, though, are made of solid wood, which produces a richer and more resonant sound. These guitars also get better with age!

The tops of acoustic guitars are most commonly made of spruce or cedar, while the woods typically used for the back and sides are rosewood, mahogany or maple. There is, however, a shift away from these woods as manufacturers search for more sustainable options, including using synthetic materials.

Taylor Guitars make some of their guitars our of Urban Ash, which is a tree that grows widely in California and is cut down periodically. There are roughly 140 million trees in California and this species of tree previously ended up as fire wood, but has now been shown to provide a good tone wood for guitars, thereby using something that was previously a wasted resource.

Well done them I say!

TOP WOODS

SPRUCE

This is the most common choice for an acoustic guitar top. It offers an excellent strength-to-weight ratio, which makes it possible for the top to be relatively thin, whilst also being strong and very resonant. Spruce tops remain responsive even when played very hard. Spruce is perfect for both strumming and finger picking styles.

CEDAR

This wood is a darker shade to Spruce and has a slight reddish colour. Cedar responds nicely to a light picking and is an excellent choice for finger picking and lower tension tunings. Cedar can, however, be overdriven if played too hard, because it is softer and not as strong as spruce. This causes the sound to compress and lose some of its clarity.

KOA

This is sometimes used as a tone wood in acoustics. It is even darker than Cedar and, given that it's very expensive, guitars featuring this wood are rare.

ROSEWOOD

This is a very dark-coloured wood, which gives a deep warmth and complex richness to the tone of a guitar. Brazilian rosewood is considered to be the top choice of tone woods and is highly prized by both guitar builders and players.

The scarcity of Brazilian rosewood, however, makes it very expensive. Indian rosewood has similar sonic qualities, but is not as attractive as the Brazilian variety.

MAHOGANY

This is an excellent tone wood, as it falls in the middle of the tonal spectrum. It gives both a bright and warm sound, whilst also providing sweet highs.

MAPLE

A maple body produces a bright, dry tone with a clear, well-defined high end. Quilted or tiger maple are favoured for their attractive appearance and are often found on the top of guitar bodies as a result.

SYNTHETICS

Guitars made using synthetics have been around for a long time and are quite popular, but it's unlikely these will ever totally replace the wooden variety. Examples of companies using synthetics are Ovation, which produces a fibreglass composite for the body and sides of its guitars, combining these with a solid wood top. Whilst the company Rainsong produces instruments that are mostly made of graphite. In general, synthetic guitars are less affected by changes in climate than wooden ones and offer distinctive tonal characteristics. On the other hand, they tend not to improve with age.

OTHER FEATURES

Guitars might feature mother-of-pearl inlays, herringbone trim or gold-plated tuners and other decorative options. Whilst these can add to the aesthetic appeal of a guitar, they do not necessarily make it a better instrument - after all the main point is that it should sound good. If it looks good too, then that's a bonus.

WHAT ABOUT THE WOOD? ELECTRIC GUITARS

In much the same way as the sound of an acoustic guitar is influenced by the choice of wood used, so the same is true for the body and necks of electric guitars, with some woods predominating. Bear in mind that low-end guitars use cheaper wood to keep the cost of manufacture down, but this often comes at the expense of tone and these woods usually do not sustain well. Higher-end guitars, on the other hand, use woods that create great tone and sustain the sound. Usually, when the guitar body feels heavy, it will hold the sound better and offer good sustain, but Alder, for example, is an exception to this general rule. The type of construction also comes into play, for example, how the neck fits onto the guitar makes a difference; indeed, some necks run through the body in order to deliver even more sustain. This is not the only factor impacting on the level of sustain, though, as clearly, the pickups (and amp) play an important role. For now, though, let's consider the types of wood typically used in the construction of guitar bodies.

Mahogany is also often used to make guitar bodies. It gives a warm tone with a lot of bottom end (bass response). Les Paul-type guitars, for example, often combine a mahogany body with a maple top. This combination gives a good tonal balance.

Maple is a tough wood and offers good tonal qualities and sustain. It is also often used as a top for the guitar body, partly because it is very attractive (quilted maple tops are an example) and partly because it can brighten a sound that would otherwise be dull. Guitar necks are also traditionally made from maple. This is in part because of its strength, and also because the material can highlight and amplify the wood used in the body of the guitar.

Basswood has a warm, balanced sound and offers great mid-range and good sustain. It is soft and easy to work with, but this means that it also dents easily. It doesn't offer much in the way of a grain or colour, so isn't very interesting appearance-wise. As a result, it's usually used on instruments with an opaque finish.

Alder used to be very popular in the 50s and 60s, and many Fender guitars from that period were made from Alder. Today it's become a more expensive wood choice, relatively speaking and isn't as common as a result. It is lightweight and has beautiful grain patterns. It offers a warm sound with plenty of highs. Instruments made from Alder tend to have less midrange and bass than instruments made from other types of wood.

Swamp Ash is being used increasingly as the wood for guitar bodies, because it is lightweight, attractive, and has a pleasant tone. Swamp Ash offers good sustain as well as firm bass tones, distinct sharp midrange, and airy highs making it a good choice for Rock or Metal players.

Korina was made popular by Gibson in the late 50s. It is beautiful, but also light, and gives a warm and balanced sound with good sustain. It's not however commonly used in production guitars these days.

Japanese Ash is not actually related to any other form of Ash, but looks similar. It is an expensive guitar wood with bright highs and midrange, good bass, and great sustain. You will be unlikely to encounter this in many production guitars.

Besides the type of wood used in the guitar body, it's worth noting that individual pieces of wood will have their own unique characteristics in terms of feel and tone. Factors influencing this can be where the tree grew, how quickly it grew, and how the wood was treated once the tree was cut down. Playing two guitars from the same brand that use the same wood for the body, the same wood in the neck and identical pickups may nevertheless have a noticeably different sound for just this reason (yet another reason to try a lot of guitars).

ARE ALL GUITARS MADE FROM WOOD?

There are some guitar manufacturers who don't use wood at all. Some make guitars entirely from Aluminium, including the necks and fret boards as well. Companies making such guitars include Drewman Guitars (UK) and AlumiSonic Aluminum Guitars (US). I've yet to try a guitar made from aluminium. Still, they are said to produce rich lows and crystal-clear highs that no other electric guitars can naturally achieve, so I will definitely be adding this to my to-do list. These guitars are not cheap though, so probably out of the budget of most people just beginning their guitar playing journey. More recently, some manufacturers have also used Carbon Fibre or other options that reduce the use of wood.

DON'T FORGET THE FRETBOARD!

The material in the neck and fretboard of the guitar is also important.

Maple A very common neck on guitars is one which in entirely made of maple, and they will typically have a bright and open sound.

Rosewood Has long been used for fret boards. It's often combined with a maple neck and softens the tone making it less bright or trebly. It is a tough and oily wood that can stand up well to extensive human contact (although can also get dirty as a result, so worth cleaning it regularly).

There are some restrictions on the sale of rosewood, so for example it's not possible to buy necks with rosewood fingerboards in the US for import into the UK, although given these are widely available for sale in the US I'm not clear how this is reducing the demand for the wood.

Ebony Is a popular wood for fingerboards as it is both beautiful and very hard. It is not seen as commonly, because it is both rare and expensive. It doesn't have the same degree of graining as rosewood, so in my view makes for a great fingerboard material and is easier to keep clean.

More recently, woods such as **Pau Ferro** and **Cocobolo** have begun to be seen in guitar necks. This is a response to the restrictions in the importation and sale of Rosewood.

As indicated above it is also possible to get necks made from Aluminium. These are light and very strong.

4

More Than Just Wood!

I've always loved the electric guitar: to hold it and work it and hear what it does is unreal.

David Lynch

We've covered the wooden elements, which make up the bulk of an acoustic, but when it comes to electric guitars, there are more components to learn about. When choosing a guitar, you should also consider the hardware. Everything from the pickups, to the type of bridge used, impacts on how the guitar will sound and feel. It's also the case that some hardware will be better suited for certain styles of music than others. For example, guitars can have pickups that are suited to a specific genre, say Rock or Metal, whilst others might be better suited to Country or Jazz.

PICKUPS

A pickup is usually a magnet with wire wrapped around it that converts the vibration of your strings into an electronic signal. Pickups can be used on both electric and acoustic instruments. The pickups in your guitar are what allows your instrument to be heard, once plugged into an amplifier of course. They're just as important to the sound of the guitar as the wood used in its construction, the strings or the amp you use, and they deserve an equal amount of consideration.

Pickups come in a range of shapes and sizes and deliver different tones; as a result, you're unlikely to use the same pickup to play Country that you use to play Rock or Metal. Selecting the right pickup for the job required is therefore important, and if this is not right, you'll find it harder, possibly much harder, to get the tone you want.

ELECTRIC GUITAR PICKUPS

Electric guitar pickups can be divided into just three main categories: Single-coil, Humbucker, and P90.

SINGLE-COIL

Single-coil pickups use a single thin magnet. An obvious example of a single-coil pickup are the ones used on a standard Fender Stratocaster (you will, however, find them on the guitars of numerous other brands). Single coil pickups don't however have one easy to define tone, largely because they're so widely used, and have developed over the years, but generally, they're considered to have more of a bright and cutting sound than humbuckers or P90s.

The genres that use single-coil pickups famously include Country and Rock, though they sound great in almost any genre. They're particularly known for their 'twang' especially when fitted in Telecaster type guitars. When fitted to Stratocaster type guitars they can have a more rounded and warm sound, with a snappier, punchier tone.

Their main weaknesses are that they tend to be quite noisy and can pick up mains hum (60 cycle hum to be precise) however, modern 'noiseless' versions tend to reduce this problem. They also don't handle very high levels of distortion very well (like you hear in Hard Rock and Metal) and this tends to be the area where humbuckers excel.

HUMBUCKER

Humbuckers are essentially two single-coil pickups working together. Humbuckers were designed to reduce or "buck" hum produced by single-coil pickups, hence the name. This was achieved by using two opposing coils. This increased the output (volume) of the pickups, but also reduced the prominence of some of the higher frequencies. This results in a richer, warmer and more powerful tone in comparison to single-coil pickups. This makes them popular with Jazz players, for example. Their higher output means that they outperform single-coil pickups in genres where high levels of distortion are required, such as Hard Rock and Metal.

P90

Finally, we have the P90s. These pickups are the happy medium between single-coil and humbucker pickups, although the P90 is technically a single-coil pickup, but one with a wide coil. This increases the area of the strings covered by the pickup, and delivers a bigger sound as a result, that is less bright than a typical single coil. The P90 is generally sought after for its relatively high output and powerful mid-range. The resulting tone can range from rich, creamy cleans to growling overdriven tones. Strangely I've only very recently tried a guitar with a P90 pick up and whilst that particular guitar didn't have a clean sound I liked much, when the distortion was switched on then the magic happened! My advice therefore is do not overlook guitars with these pickups.

ACOUSTIC PICKUPS

The key downside to an acoustic guitar is that the level of maximum volume it achieves is very low, so when played with other instruments, it really needs to be amplified somehow. There are two options - either the guitar is mic'd, or you use a pickup. Mics have the possible drawback of creating feedback, so acoustic guitars with pickups are a good solution. The pickups used can be divided into three categories: transducer, piezo and sound hole.

TRANSDUCER PICKUPS

These pickups are known for delivering a lifelike reproduction of an acoustic instrument's tone. These pickups are fixed to your instrument's soundboard and then translate its response into an electric signal. Transducer pickups do, however, have a tendency to be more sensitive to feedback than piezo or sound hole pickups.

PIEZO PICKUPS

These are also a type of transducer, but rather than being under the soundboard, they're placed under the saddle (the strip that your strings pass over). As a consequence, these pickups emphasise your strings more than the sound of your guitar as a whole, and are considered to give a more synthetic sound than soundboard transducers. Piezo pickups are, however, generally pretty resistant to feedback, so good for anyone looking to play live.

Sound hole Pickups

These pickups attach to the sound hole of an acoustic guitar. They have a definite electric-like quality to their tone, but at the more expensive end of the price range sound hole pickups actually sound really lifelike and offer a similar response to a microphone, but are less vulnerable to feedback. They are a happy medium between soundboard transducers and piezo pickups. These systems tend to be affordable and are non-invasive (meaning that they don't require any permanent modification to your guitar and indeed you can fit them yourself). They do impact on the look of the guitar though and that's not to everyone's taste.

ACTIVE AND PASSIVE PICKUPS

All three types of pickups fall under two classifications: active and passive. Active and passive pickups operate differently and have very different tones. So, to get the tone you're looking for, you should know the difference between the two.

Passive Pickups

These were the first pickups invented. They're called passive because they don't boost the signal. They have a warm and organic tone, and are very versatile handling most types of music well. The only thing they don't excel at is high levels of distortion. The vast majority of well-known guitar models available today have passive pickups installed.

ACTIVE PICKUPS

As the name implies, active pickups use active circuitry that requires a power source (usually a 9V battery) embedded into the guitar. These pickups boost your signal, resulting in a far higher output. This allows players to drive amps and distortions even harder, and more easily. This is the most common reason for using active pickups these days and is why they are typically used for Metal and Hard Rock. EMG is one of the most famous manufacturers of active pickups, and the combination of EMG 81 and EMG 85 have been widely used by famous metal guitarists including James Hetfield of Metallica.

However, the increased gain caused by active pickups can mean that the signal path, from the guitar to amp, has to be altered to accommodate this and to reduce the input gain to the amplifier, for example. As a result, for those who want to play a variety of styles, passive pickups are often a more practical option.

Tone Secrets – New Pickups

One of the easiest ways to improve the tone of your guitar is to change out the pickups for better ones! This is especially the case if your guitar is a budget model. The two electrics I use most of the time have both had a pickup swap and are better as a result. I strongly suggest getting this done by a Guitar Tech though.

GUITAR BRIDGES

Guitars are instruments that rely on the vibration of strings to produce their sound. Naturally, the strings of a guitar fix to it at the end of the neck (normally to a head) and to a bridge at the other end of the guitar on the body. There are several types of guitar bridges available, but generally they fall into two categories – electric guitar bridges and acoustic guitar bridges.

ACOUSTIC GUITAR BRIDGE

This is a relatively simple device, which is made out of a variety of wood, and in the same way as the wood or woods used in the body of the guitar these all have their own individual acoustic properties. When it comes to acoustic guitars though, the bridge does not have as much significance as the saddle. This is the material that the strings run over. Broadly speaking there a few types and these consist of ones where you can adjust the height of the strings and ones you can't. With the fixed variety, you have no way of altering the intonation of the guitar.

ELECTRIC GUITAR BRIDGE

The bridges on electric guitars are far more complex than the ones found on acoustics, and they have more unique features. Electric guitar bridges fall into two subcategories, which vary considerably from one and another. These are **Fixed Bridges** and **Tremolo Bridges**. The tremolo is also sometimes referred to as the Whammy Bar.

WHICH BRIDGE IS BEST?

The type of bridge installed on your electric guitar has a huge impact on your instrument's sound and performance, so it is worth understanding the differences between the kinds of bridges available on the market today.

Like many other aspects of a guitar's design, there is no best answer here. As with much related to the guitar, the decision is truly one of personal preference. It is worth noting that accomplished professional guitarists have employed a wide range of different bridges to get the sounds they want from their guitars. It is therefore worth trying the various options available to see which one is best for you.

FIXED BRIDGES

The most widespread and simple of electric guitar bridges is the fixed variety. It's a basic device consisting of a metal plate that's bolted to the guitar body with six individual metal saddles for each string. It allows you to adjust the length and/or height of the string, and that's more or less it. The biggest benefit of fixed bridges though is the fact that they stay in tune well and are arguably better in terms of delivering sustain.

There are two major types of fixed bridges. Fender's hard-tail, which is what you can find on some varieties of Stratocaster (although the tremolo variety is far more common) and a Tune-O-Matic Bridge made popular by the Gibson Les Paul. You can then find other variations which derive from these two bridge types.

TREMOLO BRIDGES

These are more complicated than fixed bridges due to their ability to shorten or lengthen the strings on demand. This type of bridge pivots around a mechanism that is hard fixed to the body of the guitar. This will either be a series of 6 screws or 2 posts. There are two key types of tremolo bridges that have become popular. These are Fender's synchronised tremolo and the Floyd Rose.

The synchronised tremolo relies on a set of screws and springs to pivot on the body. One major drawback of the synchronised tremolo bridge is its inability to remain in tune for a long time. After a while, all the increasing and decreasing of tension through use of the tremolo tends to pull the strings out of tune.

Floyd Rose, on the other hand, is a significantly more complex and enhanced version of the synchronised tremolo. This does a great job of locking the guitar into tune using a clamp-like device at the nut of the guitar combined with a sturdier design of the bridge itself. Its ruggedness allows the player to use the tremolo over a longer period of time and with greater gusto, without having to worry that the instrument will go out of tune – this is it's USP! The major drawback with this variety, however, is the complexity of the unit, which make any kind of adjustments or string replacement a very delicate and fiddly job.

BRIDGES - OTHER CONSIDERATIONS

If you are a beginner, there is nothing wrong with a fixed bridge. You may feel like you need the flexibility of a tremolo (or whammy bar), but it is worth considering the extra hassle that goes with it and whether it's worth it. If you plan on using several alternative tunings, for example, then it might be best to avoid a locking tremolo, as you'll need to unlock the strings using an Allen Key every time you want to change your tuning. A fixed or Fender-style bridge will therefore be a more user-friendly and less time-consuming proposition.

Tone Secrets - New Saddles or a Whole New Bridge

If your guitar is of the Strat-variety you can switch out the bent steel saddles for the block variety, which will give the guitar more sustain. Even better will be to switch out the existing vibrato block for a non-leaded steel replacement (the stock item is usually made from zinc or leaded-steel). This will add sustain, depth and improve the general tone.

I've recently done this myself on one of my guitars and I was expecting it to make a marginal difference, but it made a HUGE difference - this is really worth doing.

For the record, I opted for the Gotoh GE1010TS Vintage Tremolo System - a top quality unit and I'm a big fan of their products.

WHAT ARE GUITAR POTS AND CAPS?

Essentially these are some of the electronic gubbins inside the guitar. Put simply the Pots (which is an abbreviation to avoid saying 'potentiometers' all the time) are the devices behind the volume and tone knobs of the guitar. The Caps (capacitors) on the other hand are small devices that make up some of the other wiring within the guitar.

So, what do caps do? Well, these are used to change specific frequencies and therefore, to shape the tone. The tone pots and capacitors combine to create a low-pass filter i.e. the degree to which low notes pass through. How this is integrated into a guitar's wiring scheme adds another dimension to the manipulation of your tone. Largely the differences in caps lead to the amount of treble that comes through, so some result in a bright tone, and some give a darker tone. When buying a guitar, it might be of interest to know what value pots and caps have been installed (this is assuming the person selling the guitar knows the answer!), but it is far from critical.

Whilst clearly you can see the volume and tone knobs on the guitar body the pots and caps are hidden away within the body of the guitar. They are if you like a set feature of the guitar and it's only later that you might want to change them out if they start to fail. Alternatively, you might want a slightly different sound, which can be the result of changing the pots and caps, but for the purposes of buying your guitar I wouldn't worry about the intricacies of these two items. They do contribute to the sound, but for now, that can be your main focus, i.e. the sound the guitar makes and whether it feels like the right one to you.

For future reference though, it's worth knowing the symptoms of bad pots, which is when you hear a scratchy or static type noise coming from your amp when you turn a knob, or if the knob does not feel smooth when you turn it. The solutions to this are either replacement (use a guitar tech) or sometimes you simply need to clean the pot. If you choose to do this make sure that you use a specially designed electronics contact cleaner and protect your guitar's finish, which could otherwise be damaged by the lubricant. **Do NOT use bulk standard WD40 for this job.** The company do now also offer an electronics contact cleaner under the same brand (I use this) but other brands are available!

5

Let's Talk Money!

If you pick up a guitar and it says
'take me I'm yours'
then that's the one for you.

Frank Zappa

LET'S TALK MONEY!

So, now we've covered the features of guitars and what they're made from and the various merits of the two main guitar types of acoustic and electric. It's time to start talking about the buying process. Let's start with the money!

Top Tip - Buy the Guitar, Not the Brand

The two biggest brands in the guitar world, Fender and Gibson, are aspirational for many beginners (they were for me too). The budget guitars by both brands do not however compare well to other brands at the same price point in my opinion. Therefore, the lesson here is whether buying an acoustic or an electric - don't be seduced by the brand!

BUDGET FOR AN ACOUSTIC GUITAR

As stated previously, the key benefit of an acoustic guitar is that it is an all in one solution to your guitar playing needs! Once you've decided how much money you have to play with the bulk of this can go on the guitar (I'd suggest you also budget for a case, so it doesn't get damaged). Clearly, I don't know how flush with money you are, so I'm going to set out several price ranges to give you an idea of what you can expect to be looking at based on the various price points. I'll also give you an idea of new versus old, which I will be covering later on in this book.

Budget/Entry Level (Starting at £35/$42)

Absolutely as low as you can go short of stealing a guitar (I don't recommend this incidentally).

This will be a Spanish/Classical guitar with nylon strings and is what I learnt on many decades ago. You could probably pick one up in a garage sale, charity shop or on-line for less than this, but this is already very cheap, so I'd suggest sticking with buying new at this price point.

Low Budget (Starting at £100/$120)

This will give you a choice between steel string and nylon string. There might not be much perceptible improvement in tone between the Budget/Entry level variety above and ones in this price bracket, although playability might be a bit better, as will the quality of the build and potentially the wood used.

Medium Budget (Starting at £350/$420)

Not surprisingly there is far more choice at this price point, and you should get access to big name brands (should this be important to you). The build quality will be fairly good at this price point and the tone of at least some of these guitars will be quite good.

High Budget (Starting at £1,000/$1,200)

We're into serious money territory and the guitars at this price point the build quality should be very good with the producer using some of the best materials and should all sound great making the decision more about personal preference.

Money No Object! (Starting at £3,000/$3,600)

This is a huge amount of money! It will buy you a boutique guitar that you can own and enjoy for the rest of your life, but this is a major investment and unless that is partly what you have in mind, i.e. the instrument as an investment for the long term, I would wait for a few years before spending on this level.

BUDGET FOR AN ELECTRIC GUITAR

As above here are some price ranges to give you an idea of what you can expect to be looking at based on the various price points. Again, I've included comments about new versus old, which I will be covering later on in this book.

With electric guitars, you need to bear in mind that you will need an amp. Some beginners are put off buying an electric guitar, because they think it will be louder than an acoustic. Whilst it's true that electrics can be extremely loud, it's usually possible to play them quietly (although not in the case of my 100W Marshall valve amp!). For the most part though, practice amps can generally be played at relatively low volumes. They often also include headphone jacks, allowing you to play silently, which your household might appreciate, particularly when you're going over a lick or run for the 19th time! Bear in mind also that electric guitars are just as versatile as acoustics, if not more so, and can be used for many styles of music, from Jazz to Heavy Metal and everything in between.

Budget/Entry Level (**Starting at £150/$175 including amp!**)

We're immediately out of the budget/entry-level starting point for the acoustic above. The good news, however, is that there are a few all-in-one packages produced by some of the big name brands that can provide you with a starter kit of guitar and accessories including the all important amp that can get you up and running for an extremely low price, thanks to these being sourced from low-cost countries (I'm guessing China and other parts of the Far East in most cases). The build quality might not be the best, but they are perfectly serviceable, so if you want an electric guitar combo and don't mind have a generic 'S-type' guitar shape then this is worth serious consideration.

Some worth considering are:

Yamaha Pacifica (£299/$360 including amp)

Renowned for the quality of their instruments, the Pacifica guitar is a good option as a starter guitar. This pack consist of 20w modelling amp, cable, strap, spare strings, string winder and pick. The guitar features HSS (Humbucker, Single, Single) pickup configuration giving a great variety of available tones. This is paired with a high-quality Line 6 Spider amplifier, which allows you to customise your tone (it has over 200 amp sounds and countless effects).

This is an impressive starter pack, but it's not the cheapest option available.

Squier Affinity Stratocaster HSS Pack, Candy Apple Red £249/$300 including amp)

Here you get an iconic looking guitar, which really looks the business, being finished in a glorious deep red with a black pick guard. It also features the HSS (Humbucker, Single, Single) pickup configuration and has a comfortable maple neck with a laurel fingerboard. It comes with a Fender Frontman 15G Amp as well as a case, strap, cable and 3 months of on-line Fender lessons to get you going. This set up is going to have you looking like a Rock God right from the off! It seems a perfect starter pack to me. Given this also includes 3 months of on-line lessons, this is a good option to get you up and running.

Gear4Music LA Select Electric Guitar and Amp Pack (£139.99/$168 including amp!)

This includes 15w amp, gig bag, lead, spare strings and even a guitar pick! The guitar also features HSS (Humbucker, Single, Single) pickup configuration giving a great variety of available tones and has a modern 2 post tremolo for exciting whammy bar action! I haven't played this guitar, but at this price, this is an <u>absolute steal</u> in my opinion and worth serious consideration.

Medium Budget (Starting at £350/$420 for the guitar plus £50/$75 for a micro practice amp)

Not surprisingly there is far more choice at this price point, and you should get access to big-name brands (should this be an influencing factor). This is also a good price point to be looking at within the second-hand market, as some very decent guitars will crop up here. For new guitars you'll probably need to spend closer to £500/$600 to get a good guitar and probably not one from the big brands (and incidentally there is nothing wrong with it not having a name on the headstock that starts with F or G!). You'll need to buy the amp separately, so whilst I've included a possible budget here, I'll cover this in more detail separately below.

High Budget (Starting at £1,000/$1,200 plus £150/$180 for a practice amp or £500/$600 for a gigging amp)

Similar to the acoustics we're now into serious money territory, but this is where the section of electric guitars expands significantly, assuming you're shopping for new. At this price point, the build quality should be very good. The choice of pick up combinations will expand, meaning the variety of guitars used for different genres is broader. If you're considering the second-hand market you should be able to pick up a very good guitar in decent condition at around this price point.

Money No Object! (Starting at £3,000/$3,600 and £1,000/$1,200 for a quality or boutique amp or £2,000/$2,400 for a gigging amp)

This is a huge amount of money! It will buy you a boutique or custom shop guitar that you can own and enjoy for the rest of your life, but this is a major investment and if you have forked out this kind of money on a guitar, you're probably going to want to match it with a high-quality amp – even more money! I'd wait for a few years before spending on this level though.

NOW FOR THE AMP!

You have settled for an electric guitar – it is The One! Great news, but without an amp, it's going to be extremely quiet. Let's talk amps!

Just as guitars fall into two broad camps (acoustic or electric) so amps have two key varieties, which are transistor or valve amps. These relate to how the amp...well amplifies! The valve technology came into being first. It is still around however as it has an important characteristic that many seasoned guitarists cherish. This is that the sound can be very smooth, but when cranked up (made louder) the sound begins to break up and become increasingly distorted and compressed. This is the key sound in very many rock bands from the 1960s (think Clapton and Hendrix) through to the present day (think...well pretty much any Rock band to be honest!).

Transistors can reproduce this distortion to an extent, but it is not the same for the most part. More recently, manufacturers have used digital processing to model the distortion and this is capable of reproducing it with significant success. These modelling amps however often fall down on their ability to produce clean i.e. undistorted tones.

Whilst valve amps can sound great, they have a few drawbacks. They tend to sound at their best played loud. When the volume is cranked up, the valves are working harder and are hotter, and this makes them sing! Fantastic and really fun, but if you are playing at home this will not necessarily endear you to those nearby, be it in your house or slightly further afield! You will therefore probably want to move your amp somewhere, where it can be played loud, such as a rehearsal studio. At this point you will encounter drawback number 2 – they can be incredibly heavy! Transistor or modelling amps are far lighter. Something worth considering if you are going to be moving the amp around a lot.

It is also worth considering the format of the amp. Again, there are two varieties. You can either opt for a combo that includes both the amp and the speaker in one unit or go for separate heads (the amp) and speaker cabinets. The advantage of combos is that not only are these an all-in-one solution, but the speakers should have been matched for best effect to the amp by the manufacturer, so they should sound good too. If you mix and match this might be a bit more hit and miss, unless you opt for the two separate elements from the same brand. One advantage of a separate cabinet is that it can contain more speakers than a typical combo and therefore spread the sound, e.g. the common 4x12 cabs, these include four 12 inch speakers.

Another factor in amp development of late has been the improvements in speaker technology. In the old days, any amp had to more or less have a speaker of either 10 or 12 inches in diameter, but these days far smaller speakers are capable of producing killer sound. This is great news when it comes to considering a practice amp, as this means it will take up far less space, and you can easily carry it around with you should you wish to do so. I've recently discovered that Celestion have developed a single 12-inch speaker cabinet that is small and light due to its design, but capable of handling 250 Watts of power. That's compact, but could be seriously loud!

Top Tip - Quality Amps Help

A good amp is a leveller, so even low-end guitars can be made to sound good through them, whereas cheaper amps can offer less definition and a more 'mushy' effect overall. Higher quality amps do however tend to highlight any weakness in playing technique.

Budget/Entry Level (Starting at £50/$60 for a micro practice amp)

This will get you a micro practice amp. They might be small size, but they work really well for practicing, and some of the slightly higher cost models have built-in effects making them pretty good value and a great option for a beginner. I've rarely if ever seen these for sale second hand, so given they're inexpensive, I'd buy a new one.

Medium Budget (Starting at £150/$180 for a larger practice amp)

Fortunately, there are a whole load of amps at this price point that are capable of producing a decent sound. They will, however, fall squarely into the practice territory, so if you have any longer-term ambition to get up on stage, you'll need something with a bit more grunt. You might be able to pick one up second-hand, and as these are unlikely to have been thrashed at gigs, the chances are that the speaker will be OK.

High Budget (Starting at £500/$600 for an amp suitable for gigging)

At this price point, you will be able to get a decent combo, including from a brand name, providing you're prepared to look in the low wattage range, e.g. say 15-25 watts. This can, however, include valve amps, so don't take low watts as necessarily meaning low volume.

Some of these amps will be capable of handling a small gig. If looking at the amp and speaker separately bear in mind that heads tend to come in at a fairly high price point (typically £500/$600) so when added to a speaker cabinet, this is quite a high-cost option. Having said that it is possible to pick up heads and cabinets together second-hand at this price point, so that can be worth considering. When buying cabinets or combos second-hand you need to ask if they have been gigged, because if so the speaker might be past its best. Listen to the quality of the tone delivered by the combo or cabinet using a fairly loud clean tone and see if you can detect any break up in the sound, if so this would be one to politely decline.

Money No Object! (Starting at £1,000/$1,200 for a quality or boutique amp for home use or £2,000/$2,400 for a gigging amp)

Well at this price point you have the choice of some extremely sweet amps and speakers. The question is do you really need a 100W amp and two 4x12 cabinets or a boutique Class A combo? But hell, why not if you have the money!

Top Tip - Match your guitar to the amp so the combination works together.

The key take out from this section, is that there are a whole host of electric guitars and amps to choose from and, unless your budget will only stretch to the all-in-one solution stated earlier, you have a great variety of combinations to work with. Some of these will sound great! But some will not and some will just not have 'that sound' that you want to produce. So, once you have settled on the right guitar for you, it's worth trying it through a number of amps to find the mix that works well for you.

I'd always suggest using your guitar when testing amps, as the ones available from the shop, or if buying second hand from the seller, may sound and feel very different to your own Axe.

Tone Secret - Finding the Sweet Spot on an Amp

I've only recently discovered this, and it does seem to work, so I'm passing it on to you for you to try out. This works particularly well for valve amps, but might work with transistor amps as well (I don't have one to try to know for sure).

Set all the tone controls to 12 o'clock on the dials. Then starting with the treble take it down to zero and whilst playing something move the dial until you find the point on the dial where there is the most difference. For example, you may find that when you turn it slowly up, there is a subtle difference between 6 and 7 but after 7 there is very little change. In this case, set the dial somewhere between 6 and 7. Then repeat the process for the Middle and Bass, assuming your amp has both. You can then also do this with the Volume if the amp has a Master Volume. You may find this takes a bit of playing with to get right. Still, when you find the sweet spot, it becomes a useful reference point (indeed you might not want to change it, but use your guitar's tone controls instead to alter the tone).

Remember, though that the sweet spot ultimately is what sounds good to you. The above is merely a way to assess that the amp is working at its optimum.

Tone Secret – How to Dial in the Van Halen 'Brown Sound'

Van Halen achieved his sound by driving his valve amps really hard. These were originally Marshall's, but later he switched to using the Peavey 5150, which was developed to Eddie's spec. In your case you really need a valve amp for this and then it's just a question of turning everything to 10 (or 11 if you're Spinal Tap!). This includes all the Tone Controls and the Volume/s. Eddie then used a Variac to manipulate the power level, as a means of controlling the volume level of his amps. Hopefully your amp will have a master volume, which will allow you to control the volume i.e. don't set this one on 10 unless you want to play very loudly!

Adopting this approach resulted in the valves (tubes) in Eddie's amps running hotter than usual and this in turn provides a level of warmth and saturation from the amp, but significantly shortens the life span of the valves.

So, one to use in moderation unless you want to change your valves on a regular basis!

WHAT ELSE DO YOU NEED FOR AN ELECTRIC GUITAR?

A CABLE

First up you're going to need a cable to connect the guitar to your amp. A general rule of thumb is to always buy the best cable you can afford. These will allow a good strong signal to get from your guitar to the amp, so the tone will be better and they're also likely to last longer.

Top Tip – Don't scrunch your cable up!

Wrap your cable in a circle when you store it, because if you scrunch it up (for example by tying a knot in it) you can break the wires contained in it and this will adversely affect your sound.

PICKS/PLECTRUMS

Get some picks (AKA plectrums). These are very cheap, so it's worth getting a variety in **thin**, **medium** and **heavy** gauges. They work well in different circumstances, so thin ones are good for strumming, medium ones work well for both strumming and lead, and heavy ones are good for lead, but take a bit more practice when playing rhythm. The medium gauge pick (0.7mm) is the all-rounder and the best place to start in my opinion. You should try them all and find the one that works for you. I've gravitated towards heavy picks (1mm plus) in recent years and these work really well for Rock and Metal. A heavy pick is also great for lead playing. This is because there is less movement in the pick, which means that it is ready to hit the next note faster than a more flexible pick and so gives you greater control. On the other hand, if I'm playing an acoustic, I'm opting for a medium gauge pick.

GET A STRAP

If you want to stand whilst playing, you'll need a strap. It should be strong and comfortable and shouldn't slide around on your shoulder. Get strap locks too. These stop the strap from coming off the guitar to avoid your pride and joy from crashing to the floor. I use D'Addario Dual-Lock strap locks, which work really well, do not require any alteration to the guitar and are very inexpensive (£3.99/$5.00).

GET A TUNER

Whether you choose an electric guitar or an acoustic, a tuner is **essential!** You can spend a small fortune (or a big one) on a guitar, but if it ain't in tune, it's going to sound dreadful! It's also vital that you learn what being in tune sounds like and if you're not in tune to start with, that's not going to happen! Clip-on tuners that attach to the head of the guitar are inexpensive (I use a Snark one, as well as using their great picks). Whatever variety you opt for, it should include a display to show when the string is in tune and is a 'must-have'!

GET A MUSIC STAND

Not very glamorous I accept, but crucial in my opinion. You need to get a decent solid one. I use a **Stagg MUS-C5 T Orchestral Music Stand £19.49/$23.50)** but other similar ones are widely available.

Make sure you **don't** purchase the flimsy chrome music stand variety. These are just too weak for anything other than a few sheets of paper and the chances are you will want the music stand to hold books or a tablet, so they need to be robust. In addition, look for a music stand that has screw knobs for adjusting the height and angle of the music holder. I previously had one that used a plastic lever, but this just snapped, rendering the music stand useless and I had to throw it away!

GET A TABLET

Now you have something to put music on you're going to need a music source. This could be music books with chords and/or TAB or for a more interactive experience use a tablet and sign up to a music app such as Songsterr or GuitarPRO, or one of the guitar courses suggested in this book, or better still both! The beauty of programmes like Songsterr is that you can slow down the music to a tempo that suits you, whilst you're learning the tune. They also often include all the relevant guitar parts, so you can see all the chords, rhythm and lead parts.

AND A GUITAR STAND

It's a good idea to have your guitar instantly available on a guitar stand. There are several reasons for this. Firstly, it will remind you to play it regularly, which is a good thing. Secondly, guitars also prefer being in the open rather than cooped up in a case, which means they adjust to the temperature and humidity of their surroundings, and so require less tuning. And finally, guitar stands are also good because they will stop the guitar from falling over! This may sound obvious, but knocking guitars over and watch them crash to the floor is surprisingly easy and they don't appreciate the experience, which could cause them serious damage, such as breaking the neck (most likely where the head attaches to the neck, which is a weak point).

I've recently invested in an excellent guitar stand (**from Hercules**) which has a weight-sensitive catching device, so that when you place the guitar in it, two small arms come across the neck to stop it from falling out – ingenious! I cannot think why I didn't buy something like this years ago. I can now have at least one of my guitars on display at any one time, and it will be useful in the rehearsal studio when I need to put the guitar to one side without knocking it over. Other brands are available, of course, but in my opinion as the owner of one, Hercules offer really well designed and built stands for a reasonable price.

USE A METRONOME

You might not need to buy this! There are some available as Apps, so if you have a smart phone this is a possibility. There are also drum beat apps that can serve the same purpose and make things sound more band-like. Better still, some of the play-along song Apps, such as Songsterr or GuitarPRO, will help to keep you in time and also have a function that allows you to slow the song down to a tempo that suits you, which is really great when you're learning a new song.

6

Where to Shop

You can't buy happiness,
but you can buy guitars,
and that's sort of the same thing.

Anon

Right, so you have a handle on the money, how much you have to play with and what that is likely to buy, but now the question is <u>where</u> to buy your guitar? You have various options, let's start with the most obvious.

BUY FROM A GUITAR STORE

Buying on-line might be slightly cheaper, but in my opinion, you need to 'feel' the instrument and find one that feels right to you. There are bound to be one or more guitar stores near you, and this is a good place to start. These tend to have a large selection of guitars and to be well-stocked. This is helpful because it is good to try a decent number of guitars, not just one or two and not all of the same type, as you might surprise yourself and find that the right guitar for you was not the one that you originally expected.

Play a load of guitars yourself if possible and see what you like the feel of. Alternatively, bring along someone who can play a bit. Any self-respecting guitar store will let you try the guitars they have on display, but remember to <u>ask</u> before taking a guitar down to try it (this is just polite) and if you are relatively new to guitar or a complete beginner then it's best to ask to play the guitars in your price bracket rather than mauling one of their custom shop models! Stores can even get in guitars for you to try that are nominally on their books, but 'at the warehouse'. I suspect this means they need to order them in from the relevant wholesaler. Given the hassle factor for them in doing this, I would only suggest doing this if you are serious about the guitar or guitars in question. Indeed, you may need to place down a deposit for this service, so think carefully about this.

What if you can't yet play? Well, guitar stores are usually mainly staffed by people that play guitar, so getting them to play the guitars you're interested in is certainly an option. If doing this get them to play the same thing on the guitars to make it easier for you to compare them. Another option is to bring along a guitar-playing friend if you have one and get them to do the playing for you. This also has the advantage of providing you with a second opinion, and the chances are their skill level will be closer to yours once you've been playing for a year or so than the store guys who are usually very good. You can, of course, get both a store guy (they usually are male, I don't know why) and your mate to play the guitars. A good way to really hear how a guitar sounds is to listen from a distance of a few feet away. A guitar heard in this way will sound different than it does when you play it sat next to the amp and is what anyone listening nearby will hear.

Even better however is if you can master a few simple open chords (well not even master really, but just play, so they sound half-decent). **See also the section on Learning to Play**. E Minor (Em) and A Minor (Am) are good places to start or even just Em then move it down a string, so you fret the D and the G strings on the second fret (this is technically an Asus2 if you're interested, and actually this stuff matters later on in your guitar playing adventures). Anyway, just playing a few chords will help you to get a feel for the guitar. Consider these points:

- Does it feel good in your hands? This will tell you that the neck suits the size of your hand (usually your left one, unless ironically you are left-handed as stated earlier).

- How heavy is the guitar? Even if it is very heavy, this won't be an issue for the most part as most of your practice will be done sitting down, but later on, if you get to gig you will be standing up with it strapped to you and then you might regret buying a very heavy guitar!

- How large and wide is the guitar? Does your playing arm rest comfortably on the body?

- How complicated is it to use? Are the controls simple to use, and do they actually alter the sound!

- Can you get some nice sounds out of your 2 chords by playing with the various pickup combinations and altering the tone knob?

It's also worth considering whether the guitar sounds good played unplugged (usually a good indication it will sound good through an amp) and when played clean, as well as distorted (some guitars will sound good played clean, but not so great when distortion is added and vice versa). Of course, if you only plan on playing clean or distorted, this won't matter, but the chances are that having the option will make you a more versatile player.

Don't be afraid to ask the store assistants for advice on the guitars you're interested in – that's what they're there for after all and now you have the information from this book you will hopefully understand what they're talking about.

When choosing your guitar focus on what it is that YOU like, not the brand or what your mates are saying - if it doesn't feel right to you then it isn't the right guitar, and you need to keep looking. Have in mind that the sound you like is subjective - it's your money, and ultimately it's your call. If you like the guitar, that's all that matters.

Top Tip - Specialist acoustic guitar stores

You should consider specialist acoustic stores when shopping for an acoustic. They are more likely to have knowledgeable sales staff and will probably hold a wide selection of guitars, including more unusual brands that you are less likely to see in a standard guitar store. They do however tend to cater for experienced players, so their stock tends to be more towards the high end price-wise.

Bear in mind that this might be you first guitar, but it will probably not be your last, so in the future you will be able to upgrade or add to your collection with a guitar that might be better for a different genre of music for example.

A guitar store will be able to set up your guitar once you've bought it so that it plays optimally for you. I'll cover this in more detail later.

Top Tip – Guitar Action

When you have a guitar that interests you check the action – ideally the strings shouldn't be more than 3 or 4 mm from the neck at 12th fret; otherwise, you'll find it hard to play.

CHECK THE RETAILER HAS A GOOD RETURNS POLICY

It is possible that even after all your best endeavours, you might discover that there's a problem with your chosen guitar. Or even worse you might decide after a few days that playing the guitar just isn't for you (I sincerely hope not). Should this arise, it's helpful to know that the retailer you buy from has a reasonable policy regarding returns, exchanges, and refunds. You should therefore check this in advance before you part with your hard-earned cash.

Top Tip - Avoid ¾ size guitars

I don't recommend buying a ¾ size guitar, even for children. There are plenty of amazing videos of very young children playing incredible stuff on full-size instruments (see Sungha Jung playing Come Together on YouTube, for example). I started guitar when I was 10 on a full-sized guitar despite my fairly small hands, and it didn't prove an issue for me. If anything, it taught me how to stretch my fingers. So, unless you're buying a guitar for someone who is 8 years old or younger stick to a full-sized guitar. There are anyway far more to choose from, and it will also avoid having to buy another guitar when the ¾ size guitar has become too small.

The only exception to this rule that would be worth considering for a younger player is the Blackstar Carry-On. This is in fact a travel guitar, but as it has a short neck (only 18 frets) and small body would be suitable for a younger player. It also feels like a full-sized guitar to play and given its main purpose is as a travel guitar, it's highly portable, so good for taking around to friends' houses. It comes with a deluxe option that includes not only a gig bag, but also a Blackstar Fly 3 Bluetooth mini amp and other accessories. It's £419.00 or $502.00 so probably more what I'd call good value, rather than an out and out bargain.

BUYING SECOND HAND

Buying a pre-loved guitar can be a great option if you're on a budget and the money you save on the guitar can be used to get it professionally set up. This can be a great option if you're feeling sufficiently confident that you know what you want and can spot a good guitar. It is often the case that older guitars generally mature and sound better with age and given they lose a lot of their value once they're out of the shop they can also be great value for money, not to mention the fact that they are often offered for sale with a guitar case and other goodies. Bear in mind though that they'll be no taking it back if there is subsequently a problem with it or you change your mind.

Guitars are however relatively straightforward instruments, so providing the action feels good, and that the neck isn't bowed (look along the neck from the side to see if it is arching due to the tension of the strings, i.e. if the gap at the 12th fret is more than at the 21st fret there is an issue) and the pots aren't making a bad scratchy noise, and most importantly the guitar feels good in your hands, plays well and sounds great – then you might just have a bargain.

HOW TO BUY A USED GUITAR

The following are a few guidelines for purchasing a used guitar:

Check the make, model and condition of the guitar in advance. This will allow you to do some research on it. You can also check reviews to see what other people think of the guitar. In addition, check out a number of ads - don't just go for the first one. What is the market rate for this guitar based on different conditions (like new, slightly worn, battered etc.)? This will give you a benchmark price to work from to assess whether the price being asked for the guitar is a fair one. The same thought process applies to amps, of course.

Ask the seller about the age and condition of the guitar. In particular, you can ask them how long they've had the guitar and what repairs or maintenance it's had. They should be upfront with you on things like scratches or pots that need changing, for example. Asking this may also show that some of the guitar is no longer original, as certain parts might have been changed. This might include the pickups, which could be beneficial, so changes are not necessarily a bad thing.

Today there are a whole host of places to search on the Internet (this is covered later). Choose a seller who's local if at all possible, so that you can check out the guitar in person before buying it. You can't rely completely on the description of the guitar in terms of its condition and whilst clearly, a photo is helpful, it's best to see it in person, but even more importantly, as I've been stressing throughout this book, you need to play it.

Give the guitar a once-over. The chances are that you're going to have to accept a bit of wear and tear, unless it's not been out of the box and is pristine (these do come on the market, but the discount is likely to be less than a guitar that's been played a bit). The things to look for are scratchy pots (they might need replacing) very worn frets (they will probably need replacing) tuners that are very loose (again they might need replacing). Look at the condition of the strings if they look very dull they're almost certainly old, and this will impact on the tone making it similarly dull, so if you decide to buy the guitar installing a new set of strings will immediately brighten the sound.

Try playing the instrument. Play all the kinds of music and sounds you normally do on a guitar. If you are able to bend strings, bend them and check out the sound as well as trying other techniques that you know. Pay particular attention to all of the frets of the guitar, not just the ones you usually play. Pay special attention to the ones at the body end of the fretboard. Start playing all frets from the Low E string to the High E and listen for any strings that sound odd or rattle. If you hear a noise, this might be a string with broken windings rattling. If it is not this, however, then it is likely to be a fret. This can indicate that the guitar is improperly set up. This might not be the end of the world, but could indicate you'd need to spend more money getting the guitar set up correctly (something to use in your negotiations on price).

Check that the guitar feels comfortable to play. Does the neck feel good in your hands? Is it easy to move up and down the neck? Is the fretboard too wide for your hands or even too small?

Minor scratches, cracks or chips are to be expected if the guitar has had a bit of use, but lookout for cracks that go right through the finish down to the wood. If there's a deep crack in the finish this can be a sign of separating seams within the body and structural damage can be an expensive fix, so this would be a guitar to avoid! Similarly, look for rust on the guitar. If there's any rust on the bridge, then it's worth reconsidering the purchase.

Check the action on the guitar. You should look for a consistent gap between the strings and the fretboard. If the guitar's action is bad, you can potentially adjust this yourself or get this done professionally at a guitar store, so don't let this put you off buying the guitar if it's the one for you.

On the other hand, you need to carefully inspect the neck. Look along the neck from the head to the body with one eye shut. It should look consistent along its full length. The guitar neck should be virtually straight, although a little bowing is OK. The neck joint, where the neck attaches to the body, should be good and tight (if it's not this will dramatically impact the sustain of the guitar). Evidence of a damaged guitar neck can sometimes show up in other parts of a guitar, particularly in the saddle and bridge. If a saddle and bridge have been lowered as much as possible, it can indicate that the neck of the guitar will probably need to be reset.

If you know how you can also test the truss rod (this is a metal rod within the neck that helps to maintain the correct relief on the guitar neck) to see if this allows for adjustment; if so that's a good sign. If, however, you look along the neck and see a series of hills and valleys, that's going to be expensive to sort out. Excessive forward or backward bowing tells you that the truss rod is out of adjustment, but at its worse, it will indicate that the truss rod is stripped or broken and replacing this is a major operation, so again this is probably a guitar to avoid.

Thoroughly inspect the area where the head transitions into the neck (the headstock) as this is vulnerable to damage if the guitar is dropped or takes a hit in this area. The tell-tale signs are wrinkles or ridges on and around the headstock. This will almost certainly indicate that the guitar has had a headstock repair. Even when perfectly repaired, a guitar with a broken headstock is only worth half of one that has never been broken. You may need to factor in the cost of a new neck at some point and whilst you could potentially fit this yourself this will add a good £100/$120 to your expenditure. It's also worth bearing in mind that if you plan on fitting a new neck (as I've done in the past) then the neck will almost certainly need to have holes drilled by you in order to make sure it is a perfect fit. This requires you to clamp the guitar and neck to ensure they don't move whilst you drill the holes. This is not difficult but is something that needs to be done carefully, if you're not to ruin the neck and waste the money you spent on it. If in doubt, get a guitar tech to do it is my advice.

COST

It's quite likely that a guitar bought second hand might need some repairs or a setup. Buying a guitar that needs a little work done isn't necessarily a bad thing, though, as long as you come out ahead in the end. It is, however, certainly an important factor in buying a used guitar, so don't be seduced by a low price, as it shouldn't be the only or deciding factor. Bear in mind that if something seems too good to be true, it usually is. It may even indicate that the guitar is stolen! If it has a visible serial number this is something that you can check. If the serial number has been sanded off or obscured in some other way then this is not a good sign!

GET YOUR GUITAR PROPERLY SET UP

This refers to the art of making final adjustments to the guitar in order to ensure that it plays well. When a lower-end guitar ships from the factory, it is often not set up optimally, for example, the fret edges might be sharp, the action too high or the intonation off. If the action is too high (the strings are too far away from the fretboard) it takes more effort to fret the strings, but could also be an indication that the neck is bowed (which would not be good). Here's what to look out for:

- Is there even action all the way up and down the fretboard? The strings should sit slightly higher at the 12th fret.

- Check for fret buzz by playing chords and single notes at different spots on the neck. If there is some fret buzz, this can probably be cured by raising the action a bit higher.

- Check the intonation of the guitar. This refers to how well a guitar is in tune up and down the neck. You can check this by playing an open D Chord and then playing the same D chord at the 14th fret. If the chord doesn't sound good at the 14th fret, it means that the intonation needs to be adjusted.

Once you're content that the guitar is the right one for you, then you can always ask the guitar store (assuming you're buying from one) to get it set up as part of clinching their sale, or if this fails you'll probably need to pay about £35/$50. When you have your guitar professionally set up, you'll get any issues with the guitar addressed as part of this service. Plus you will get a new set of strings, so your guitar will play better. This is really worth doing, and you'll know that the guitar is as good as it can be.

BUY ON-LINE

Shopping on-line for your guitar can give you more options as on-line music stores typically have a very large range of guitars to choose from. Many on-line retailers will also sell pre-loved instruments, and you can usually find options on on-line classified and auction sites. This can work well if you know with complete certainty which particular guitar you want. The prices can be attractive as well, given that these stores don't have the overheads of brick and mortar shops. There are downsides, however. The problem is that if you buy it on-line, you won't have anyone helping you, you can't discuss your needs with an expert, and crucially you can't test the guitar. Given what I've said previously about the need to find a guitar that is right for you and indeed that individual guitars of the same model and brand can sound and feel different, you will miss out on this important aspect when buying on-line. You are merely able to choose one model, spec, colour and of course, price.

I've only once been tempted by a guitar on-line, and I agonised over the buy decision for a long time, purely because I wanted to try the guitar out first hand, but this wasn't an option as the manufacturer only offered it on-line through their website. In the end, I opted to buy one. This was largely as I was seduced by the look of the guitar and its price. The guitar proved to be a disappointment initially. The colour for a start was significantly darker than shown on the website. The pickups and hardware were poor, and all things told it left me feeling considerable buyer's remorse! I subsequently had a new Gotoh floating bridge fitted, new electronics and new pickups (Iron Gear) and now have a great guitar that I really enjoy playing, but it ended up costing me substantially more than I had originally expected. So, let this tale guide you when considering buying a guitar on-line (I wouldn't ever again).

I would however not think twice about buying an amp on-line or any other bit of electronics, because in these cases they will be of a similar standard, i.e. the amp in a shop will be identical to the same model sold on-line, so providing you have tried it somewhere previously so you know how it sounds and know it is the one for you, then buying this on-line is definitely a good option. Nevertheless, it is good to support your local guitar store too, assuming you're buying new and you can and should haggle for a lower price or additional kit for free, which is not an option with an on-line store, as far as I'm aware.

If you're still determined to buy on-line then some of the options to consider are set out below (clearly this is nothing like an exhaustive list and looking through your favourite guitar magazine will almost certainly suggest many others I've missed). Location is of some significance still given there will be shipping to take into consideration. I've therefore stated the base location of the company concerned. I've not however made a distinction between new and pre-loved, which will be available on all sites with the exception of Amazon, to the best of my knowledge.

Amazon (international)

Amazon, as I'm sure you know, is the largest on-line sales platform in the world, bar none. You can buy pretty much anything on Amazon, and this includes guitars. Amazon is one of the best places to buy guitars on-line if you're looking for a beginner or intermediate level guitar. This is where they excel, because they often offer these guitars at lower prices than typical guitar stores and offer fast and free shipping if you're an Amazon Prime member. In terms of customer service they usually back the buyer, so if you have any issues with your purchase, they'll usually just refund you with no quibble.

eBay (international)

eBay is the world's largest on-line platform for buying used goods, and this includes a very good selection of musical instruments including competitively priced guitars. Buying guitars on eBay is very safe as the platform is very buyer-focused. If you feel that there was a problem with the product you ordered, you're entitled to a refund. Their money-back guarantees policy, for example, ensures that you'll be covered if you don't receive the item from the seller, the product is damaged, or even if the item doesn't match the description given by the seller.

Gear4Music (UK)

Launched in 2003 and now with 1.3 million customers, Gear4Music.com is a leading retailer of musical instruments and equipment. They have a huge range of musical equipment available from some of the biggest brands as well as offering their own great value Gear4Music music product range, which includes guitar and amp packages (one of which I've featured in this book).

GuitarGuitar (UK)

They are officially the UK's largest guitar retailer on-line and in-store. At the time of writing they have 7 shops within the UK and offer a huge selection of guitars, amps, effects and hi-tech instruments. They cover everything from a first beginner's guitar to a boutique super guitar and everything that goes with them. In my opinion, they are also one of the friendliest guitar stores in the UK with a huge selection of stock – always a joy to visit in my experience. They also usually have a guitar tech on-site, so that's a bonus should you need any adjustments made to your new Axe.

Guitar Centre (US)

Guitar Centre is one of the largest, most well-established guitar stores, but their on-line catalogue is also impressive. Guitar Centre can supply cheap beginner guitars all the way to professional quality ones. One of Guitar Centre's best perks is their used catalogue. Since they accept trade-ins at any one of their physical stores, you can purchase a used guitar from any one of their physical stores.

Professional Music Technology - PMT On-line (UK)

PMT are an award-winning musical instrument and equipment retailer established in 1991. They are now one of the largest stockists in the UK and have 16 stores across the country at the time of writing, but are expanding fast, so I would expect to see more stores in the future. They stock a wide variety of guitars and also provide some very good, informative and entertaining videos (see YouTube – search PMTVUK).

Sweetwater (US)

Sweetwater is one of the largest on-line retailers for musical instruments, gear, and software. It's one of the most reliable on-line guitar stores, offering products from all of the major brands such as Gibson, Fender, PRS, ESP and Ibanez. They also offer the budget options from each brand, such as Epiphone guitars, PRS SE, ESP LTD, and Mexican made Fender guitars.

Thomann (Germany)

Thomann is reputedly the largest on-line and mail order retailer for musical instruments, light and sound equipment worldwide. They have about 10m customers in 120 countries and 80,000 products on offer. I've purchased an amp from them in the past and found their customer service to be excellent even when handling a return – somehow I unintentionally managed to buy two of the same amp (Line6 150 AmpliFi), so one had to go back! They made the whole process as painless as it could be and didn't quibble in the slightest – highly commendable and I'd use them again. Their prices are very competitive too in my experience.

7

Looking After Your Guitar

*My guitar is not a thing. It is
an extension of myself, it is
who I am.*

Joan Jett

CLEANING

First off think about your hands. Are they clean, or do you have bits of jam on them still from breakfast? If so, you don't want that stickiness all over your guitar – wash your hands immediately! Not least because that gunk on your hands could be corrosive and this will dull the sound of your strings over time.

It's also important to wipe down your strings, fretboard and the body of the guitar for the same reason. Use a microfibre cloth for this task, although if your fingerboard is really mucky, you can use a super fine grain steel wool (0000 grade) to gently remove it, paying special attention to either side of the frets where muck tries to accumulate.

STRINGS

This is where the magic starts, so let's look after them! If you notice that the bottom of the strings look black and furry and the guitar isn't staying in tune like it used to do, it's almost certain that it's time to change your strings! Let's face it strings are cheap, so this is an investment in your tone and depending on how often you play (and for how long) they should last a fair while, so whilst professional and semi-pro guitarists might change strings every week I think I change mine roughly every 6 months and I play a lot. It's also good to have a spare set of strings, so that when it's time to change them you can do so immediately rather than wait for your next trip to the guitar shop, but you could of course order them on-line.

A few important points to bear in mind when changing strings. Why not clean your neck at the same time? When the strings are off it's significantly easier. It's advisable to not take them all the strings off at the same time as this significant reduction in tension can cause the neck to bow or warp. To avoid this just take three off at a time (I go with the A, D and G in one go and then the Low E, B and E). In a similar vein, some people recommend loosening the strings on your guitar when you're not playing it. This is sensible if you're transporting it, but generally, it is not a good idea to keep changing the tension on the neck and body. Plus, it gives you the added hassle of having to tune up whenever you want to play, so I don't recommend this.

STORAGE

It's worth considering the conditions that you will be keeping your guitars in and how this might change, for example during the seasons. Bear in mind that guitars do <u>not</u> like the following:

- Direct sunlight (unless you like a faded finish).

- Significant humidity.

- Significant heat (don't leave them by a radiator or fire) or coldness (for example in the garage during the winter).

- Significant changes in temperature, as this can cause the wood to expand and contract, which can cause damage to the instrument.

Incidentally, valve amps similarly do not appreciate any of the above either, so that's also worth bearing in mind.

Essentially, if the environment is one that you're comfortable in, for example not too hot or cold and not too humid, then the chances are your guitar and amp will like it too.

8

What About Effects (FX)?

I'm all for stage diving, but just don't step on my pedals.

Kurt Cobain

So, let's say you now have your guitar or guitars and you have gone for an electric or an electric acoustic, and you have an amp to make it loud enough to hear. You can now enter a new world of sound through the introduction of pedals. These are small boxes of magic! Not really, but they can alter your tone significantly. All you need to do is plug them between your guitar and the amp and click them on for a wealth of new sounds. Most of these boxes (commonly referred to as stomp boxes) are powered by a 9v DC battery, or you can invest in a separate power source to avoid the problem of batteries dying when you are in the midst of one of your finest moments as a guitarist.

Effects come in two distinct types – multi-effects units or individual pedals. For those starting out on the guitar a multi-effects unit can be a good option. These will as the name suggests contain a number of the key effects all in one convenient box. You therefore only need to put this in between the guitar and the amp and you're off and running. They will also work out as a relatively inexpensive way to introduce FX into your guitar playing arsenal. They do however have a couple of downsides namely that they can be fairly complicated to navigate when you want to alter the effects and whilst some of the effects will be great some might not be so good. The effects themselves will be digital rather than analogue, so can sometimes sound synthetic, which isn't to everyone's liking.

The alternative is to buy individual stomp boxes. This will allow you to tailor your sound more finely using the individual character that each pedal has. There are literally hundreds of pedals to choose from and they tend to be more intuitive to use than the multi-FX option. The downside here however is that the cost can mount up quite a bit given that even the cheapest pedals will be around the £50/$60 mark and many are substantially more with some in the £300/$360 region. The whole area of pedals also has a further downside, which is that it can become an obsession with guitarists striving for the perfect combination in order to reach sonic nirvana! This can in itself become a distraction from the art of actually playing guitar, so be careful to find a balance.

Let's take a look at some of the most common pedals, and as with guitars you should try a number of them and see which ones work for you. Broadly these are the main categories of effects:

- **Wah**

- **Dynamic Effects** – Compressor, Boost, Equalisation (EQ) and Volume

- **Pitch-shifting Effects** – Octavers and Harmonisers

- **Drive** – Overdrive, Distortion and Fuzz

- **Modulation** – Chorus, Phaser, Flanger, Tremolo and Vibrato

- **Delay** – Echo and Delay

- **Reverb**

DYNAMIC EFFECTS

Compression

These pedals level out the peaks in the dynamic range to make it a more consistent volume. Quiet notes are made louder and louder notes are reduced in volume. They increase the punchiness and harmonic response of your playing. Guitar players can also use this to increase the level of sustain as they will bring up the volume of a sustaining note, which is ideal for solos. They can also add the type of attack that is often heard in Country and Funk. The result delivered by these units is a smoother, less variable signal with noticeably less dynamic range than without it engaged, but a more consistent volume. They are best used with restraint.

Boost

These pedals allow you to boost the signal from your guitar into the amp without necessarily adding distortion. This is typically up to a maximum number of decibels. This can be useful for two reasons. It can drive the amp harder, making it overdrive or distort if that's your goal and/or it can increase the volume of your guitar lifting it out of the mix. This is very useful for solos, for example where you want to increase the volume of the individual notes, which might otherwise be swamped by the other instruments playing at that time.

Equalisation (EQ)

These pedals allow you to alter the extent to which certain frequencies come through, so you can therefore shape the tone of your guitar by boosting or cutting bass, middle or treble. You might use this for example to scoop out the mid-range frequencies (mids) in order to get an 80's tone or even add in more mids in order to be heard over the other instruments in the band.

Volume

Another self-explanatory pedal, which does exactly what the volume on your amp does, but in this case activated by your foot using a rocker pedal. This can be useful for both achieving the boost action that you would otherwise use a boost pedal by pressing the rocker down quickly or using it to provide a swell effect by slowly depressing the rocker pedal. This works very well when combined with reverb and delay.

PITCH-SHIFTING
Octavers

Most of these pedals will allow you to add harmony notes an octave or two octaves above or below the note being played. This can for example allow you to thicken up a tone by adding bass notes, and the effect is quite drone-like, artificial and unique sounding. They can be used to fill up the high-end frequency range (the octave above) or the mid-bass range (the octave below). These pedals can therefore be very useful and are commonly used on guitar solos.

Harmonisers

These are very similar to octavers, however in this case you get greater flexibility, as you can choose the interval to be added, so that it's not just an octave. This can work really well for distorted solos. They can also add more interest to your rhythm playing, but you probably wouldn't want to use these all the time.

Polyphonic Harmonisers

It's worth noting that most bulk standard octavers and harmonisers struggle to cope with a number of notes at the same time, such as when you want to play a chord! In this case you need a polyphonic harmoniser, because they can cope with numerous notes. In fact they sound pretty great in my opinion being able to produce some nice organ-like tones, so these would be my recommendation if you're considering any pitch shifter.

DRIVE EFFECTS
Overdrive

These pedals boost the gain to drive your valve amp into distortion and to simulate the sound of a valve amp distorting. They clip the signal, which means that the signal is compressed when it becomes distorted. This generally results in a smoother, warmer sound than that produced by distortion pedals, which we'll cover next. Overdrives still allow your guitar's tone to shine through. They work well when paired with a valve amp to provide an organic boost to your tone.

Distortion

Most guitarists make a distortion pedal their first purchase. It immediately opens up a range of sounds suited to Rock and Metal. High-gain pedals are good for producing the sound of a heavily driven valve amp at low volumes. They usually also deliver a compressed tone with sustain and harmonics. This makes them great for lead guitar lines.

Tone Secrets – Playing with Distortion

When players are starting out they can be tempted to whack the distortion on to the max, but then play rather tentatively. This does not deliver a good sound, in my opinion. Maybe I did this too in the past I can't now recall, but I've discovered that you get the best out of distortion, whether using natural distortion from a tube amp or distortion from a pedal, when you dial back the volume and hit the strings harder. Give it a try!

Fuzz

This effect dates back to the early 60s and can be heard on a number of Jimi Hendrix tracks, check out Voodoo Child as a great example and the Rolling Stones, (I Can't Get No) Satisfaction is a further example of the use of fuzz. Much like distortion pedals, fuzz pedals are able to increase sustain and harmonic overtones, which makes the sound more compressed and typically produce more warm, woolly and fat tones.

Wah

These pedals produce a...well, kind of Wah sound! This can be altered by the use of a rocker pedal, or sometimes they can be left in a mid-way point (referred to as a Cocked Wah) to make a particular sound, as used on the intro to *Money for Nothing* by Dire Straits. This effect is good for adding interest to rhythm parts and is widely used in solo work. Most famous electric guitar players that you can think of will have used a wah at some point in their career, possibly extensively

– Jimi Hendrix and Slash are just two notable exponents of this device.

MODULATION

Chorus

These provide a watery shimmer to your sound as if indeed there were a chorus of singers. This can be great for filling out your sound if used sparingly. When paired with compression and reverb, this is a sound that was widely used for rhythm parts in the 1980s and 90s including by Nirvana on *Come as you are*.

Phaser

These were very popular during the 1970s and add a psychedelic sound to your guitar. They are one of the most recognisable guitar effects available. You can hear their use in the music of Van Halen and The Eagles, to mention but two. These pedals can give an almost speech-like quality as well as other weird and wonderful sounds.

Flanger (Pronounced Flan-Jer)

Flangers produce a swirling sound and have a metallic quality to them that could be said to be rather sinister sounding and, perhaps not surprisingly, they're popular with Metal bands. Listen to Metallica as an example, but also The Police on *Message in a Bottle*.

Delay/Echo

Does what it says on the tin, or stomp box in this case. These units give a repetition of sound much like an echo. The duration of the repeats of notes can be varied in length, and in some cases, the length of notes can be set to match a musical time signature, such as dotted-eighth notes as used by The Edge from U2.

Reverb

This is replicating the effect of sound bouncing off the surfaces around you and then decaying as the sound is absorbed. Examples are Room Reverb and Hall Reverb. The larger space (the hall) will have a bigger, more open sound. Reverb is very useful in filling out your sound and making it sound more natural. Sound without any reverb is said to be 'dry'.

Reverb is in fact so helpful and widely used that the vast majority of amplifiers come with this built-in, although there are also a whole host of effects pedals available offering a wider variety of sounds than that offered by most amplifiers. Pedals will usually seek to emulate the types of reverbs possible, so will often include Room (ambient sounding) or Plate or Spring (ways in which amps typically generate reverb) as options and these all sound different.

OTHER POINTS TO NOTE

Tuner Pedals

OK, not an effect, but very important regardless. I've said that the clip-on variety work reasonably well and are inexpensive, but I suspect not the most accurate and in my experience the batteries don't last long and these are expensive! So that's something to bear in mind.

If, however, you're going down the stomp box route then having a dedicated tuner pedal would be a sensible investment. These will typically allow you to tune to any note making Drop D or other alternative tunings easier to achieve. I've also heard it said that the clip-on tuners can sometimes fly off the guitar and whilst this has never happened to me you don't want a tuner flying into the face of one of your adoring fans!

Stacking Pedals

This is the term used to describe where multiple pedals of the same variety are played at the same time, for example I have two overdrive pedals on my pedal board and when they're both on at the same time they sound awesome (IMHO!) as the two effects work together to make an even more distorted sound. This works really well for lead lines.

Pedal Boards

Let's imagine that you have invested in a range of pedals to alter your tones and have them arranged over the floor connected up, so they're all over the place and just waiting to literally trip you up. The solution is, of course, a pedal board. This is typically a metal rack, onto which you can attach your pedals and a power unit if you have one. This makes it easier to cart them around for a start, but also importantly to organise them in such a way that the signal chain works at its best (see Law and Order below).

Power Supply

All effects units, whether of the multi-FX or stomp box variety require power. In the case of a multi-FX unit this will be mains power, but stomp boxes usually run off 9v batteries or by being plugged into a power source such as the MXR iso-brick, which is the one I use, but there are many similar units on the market. The advantage of using such a power supply is that you don't need to worry about batteries dying, which would be a particular problem if you're playing live at some point.

Law and Order!

There are differing views on the 'correct' order that pedals should be placed in and there's certainly no law dictating this, however there is a generally agreed approach that certain pedals are best to go before your amp such as distortion and overdrive, and some such as delays and modulation that should go into the effects loop of your amp (if there is one included on your amp it will be on the back panel of the amp).

I've recently heard it said that placing distortions within the effects loop can even damage some amps, although I'm not sure why this should be, but probably worth checking the manufacturers manual to see if this is stated. I put my delay pedal going into the effects loop of my amp and I think that it does sound better placed there.

Anyway, here is a general order for consideration, as this is the perceived wisdom on this topic as it works well, but as

I've said there's no law here, so feel free to play with it and you could get the tone that sounds right to you by switching around the order:

Before the Amp (i.e. cable from your guitar goes into these effects and then into the input of your amp)

- **Tuner**

- **Wah**

- **Dynamic Effects** – Compressor, Boost, EQ and Volume

- **Pitch-shifting Effects** – Octavers and Harmonisers

- **Drive** – Overdrive, Distortion and Fuzz

Into the Effects Loop

- **Modulation** – Chorus, Phaser, Flanger, Tremolo and Vibrato

- **Delay** – Echo and Delay

- **Reverb**

Just for you!

If you would like my free list of the:

- Top Ten Acoustic Guitars

- Top Ten Electric Guitars

- Top Ten Amps

- Top Ten Effects

Then use the email below and this will be sent to your inbox.

stevecabain@gmail.com

Please state FREE GIFT in the subject title of your email and allow at least 2 days for me to process your request.

9

Learning Guitar
- Starting Out

Sometimes you want to give up the guitar, you'll hate the guitar.

But if you stick with it,

you're gonna be rewarded.

Jimi Hendrix

HOW SHOULD I LEARN GUITAR?

Get a teacher! This is clearly the most obvious way to begin your guitar playing journey.

PERSONAL LESSONS

Arguably the best, but almost certainly also the most expensive way to learn guitar. A lesson typically costs £35/$50, so having 2 lessons per week will start to rack up the cost. I recommend one lesson a week with plenty of practice by you in between. Having this structure and someone monitoring your progress is really helpful. If you think the first person you try is not for you then find someone else, there are bound to be numerous guitar teachers in your area.

TEACH YOURSELF

Of course, you could try going it alone. There's certainly a lot of material available on the Internet. You could probably spend a lifetime going through it all there's so much of it! However, bear in mind that you will need to approach these in such a way that there is some element of structure to what you're learning. There is a significant danger that what you end up doing turns out to be pretty random, and this is likely to be very inefficient, and you could well become demotivated. You could also learn bad habits and not have anyone's input to correct these. I, therefore, recommend going to a teacher initially and at least getting the basics down before striking out on your own. Having said that the Internet is a great place to augment your guitar playing skills, whether it's learning a specific song or a particular technique the chances are that you can find one or more videos on it. Not all of these are of the same quality, so hunt around until you find the best ones for you.

USE A GUITAR COURSE

A middle ground is to use a guitar course. There are a number of these aimed at players starting out. The good thing about these courses is they provide a logical progression taking you through the basics and on to more complicated and stretching material. Two courses I can confidently recommend are provided below. (I've no links to either of these, they are merely ones I've come across that look very good to me):

The-Art-of-Guitar course (see the-art-of-guitar.com)

This is only $10.95 per month, so very reasonable value. I'm a big fan of the teacher Mike, who makes what he teaches very accessible. Check out his YouTube videos for a sample!

Learn Practice Play (see pauldavidsguitar.com)

This is Paul Davids beginner guitar course. For one payment of $199 or three monthly payments of $79, you get lifetime access to all course materials. Paul provides 7 core modules and 55 in-depth videos, including PDFs with tabs and downloadable backing tracks. This is a well-structured course.

Next Level Playing (see pauldavidsguitar.com)

This is Paul's course for intermediate players. Again, it has 7 modules and includes tabs, downloadable backing tracks and all that good stuff for the same cost, i.e. one payment of $199 or 3 monthly payments of $79 you get lifetime access to all course materials.

In addition to the above courses, which are structured well and give you a basis for moving on with your guitar playing, there are also courses that are aimed at getting you up and running by playing songs from the off. I can't vouch for these, but four I'm aware of that would be worth exploring are:

Yousician (yousician.com)

This programme is available to players at any level of proficiency from outright beginners to more advanced players. It builds a range of skills from learning chords, strumming, melodies, lead, rhythm, finger picking and more. They offer an inventory of videos and lessons and have lots of popular songs to learn. They include Weekly Challenges to push you to enhance your skills and progress-tracking as you learn.

I'd say this is a good comprehensive offering and certainly worth consideration.

Fender Play (Fender.com)

They describe this as a portable on-line guitar school where you can learn at your own pace and play as little or for as long as you like. The lessons are delivered by world-class instructors using top quality video lessons. It's suitable for acoustic and electric guitar and allows you to learn strumming skills and songs based on your favourite genre, whether Rock, Blues, Folk, or Country.

I particularly like the fact that you can get the first 3 months free with some Fender purchases and even if you don't purchase a Fender they offer a free trial, so this is also worth considering.

Simply Guitar by JoyTunes

Again, this company offers guided video lessons as a way of learning to play guitar. This software provides real-time feedback, which is pretty neat. They aim to get you up and playing quickly, even if you have no previous experience. You can learn to play at your own pace using step-by-step tutorials, made by world-class music teachers. As with other learning apps you can learn to play your favourite songs.

This App (available from the App Store) covers guitar fundamentals and would be good for a beginner. It goes over playing chords, chord switching and strumming techniques. They even include a guitar tuner.

It has been awarded 'Editors Choice' by Apple and Best tool for beginners by NAMM[1], which is impressive. At the time of writing is scored 4.7 out of 5 from 6,968 reviews, which is pretty good going.

Justin Guitar Beginner Course

Justin's Beginners Course is an effective, enjoyable and logically structured guitar teaching method. Over one million people have apparently learned how to play guitar using his free web-based course at JustinGuitar.com, and now you can follow his lessons in an interactive format. This course offers

[1]NAMM stands for the National Association of Music Merchants and is a large annual event in the U.S.

a step-by-step learning path that includes basic chords, chord changes and strumming patterns, finger picking patterns and the use of the capo.

Justin is clearly a good guitar teacher, and indeed this app has a rating at the time of writing of 4.9 out of 5 from 2,099 reviews, which is quite frankly phenomenal! People love this App!

If I was starting out as a beginner, I would probably go for this course to get me started.

(Please note that I've no affiliation of any kind with Justin and his guitar courses, or indeed any other suppliers mentioned in this book!)

YouTube

So, the above are some good resources for learning guitar. In addition, I find it fun to watch videos from the following guys (as with guitar shop guys I'm not sure why they are typically male, but they do seem to be – if anyone can recommend a good female guitarist's channel to watch then let me know!) so when you're not practicing have a look at some of these for interest, and indeed inspiration. There are many others, so search until you find ones that you like.

- **Ben Eller** (including his wonderful - **This is Why You Suck at Guitar** series! It's not only informative, but highly amusing to boot!)

- **Steve Stine** (see also www.guitarzoom.com)

- **Justin Guitar** (see also www.justinguitar.com)

- **Budda Geudes** (see his doctor guitar YouTube channel, which is Good for gear reviews)

- **David Wallimann** (Good for tips and tricks and theory to make you a better more musical player)

- **Finger Style Club** (just discovered this channel, which is advanced, but great for learning finger style tunes)

10

What Next?

Relax. Be yourself. Play a lot.

Joe Satriani

WHAT NEXT?

Once you've decided on who's going to teach you. You need to focus on what you're learning. My advice is to KEEP IT SIMPLE initially! You shouldn't, in my opinion, obsess about shredding with insane speed (playing single notes very quickly). This in isolation is totally pointless, as far as I'm concerned. It seems to me to be the equivalent of learning to lay down an awesome serve in tennis without knowing any of the other shots, it might look impressive, but it's only part of the picture. Sure, it's worth challenging yourself with some tricky techniques, but it's good to try and become a rounded player, particularly if you ever intend to play in a band.

Things you should know when starting to learn guitar.

- Learn Whole Songs

- Keep it fun! Keep your eye on the prize!

- Practice schedule 50/50 - Playing for fun for 30 minutes to start with including playing songs or musical passages you have already learnt, ideally from memory, i.e. not looking at the music. Then 30 minutes learning about the guitar, music theory or finding videos you can learn from.

- Avoid finger pain. You can achieve this by getting the right guitar to begin learning on. As stated previously in this book, this is an electric guitar or Spanish acoustic guitar in my view. When practicing, try not to press down hard all the time. Take breaks and learn other things that don't require fingering the guitar.

Top Tip – Practice Strumming Patterns without Fretting

If your fingertips are becoming painful you can practice strumming patterns muting the strings. You can also practice shifting between chords without pressing down on the strings this helps to get the shape into your mind and builds up muscle memory.

Get through the first 2 months!

It's not about talent; it's about practicing so that you increase your skills.

You might have heard of the 10,000 hours theory. This says that you can master <u>anything</u> providing you put in 10,000 hours of learning, be it becoming a chess grandmaster or a master of the guitar!

Now I'm not suggesting that this should be your goal, but the point here is that if you put in the time and effort, you will be rewarded. Imagine, for example, if your guitar journey is just starting how much better you will be once you have been learning for 50 hours. If you do 30 minutes practice a day that would take you 100 days or just over 3 months. I suggest breaking this down, perhaps do two 15 minute sessions a day at the start. Once you've got your first 50 hours under your belt, you should largely be through the fingertip pain point, and then you can really motor!

Get your fingers on the strings! The key focus should be on playing. I read many years ago that John McLaughlin was round at Jimi Hendrix's house and they were playing guitar and John said let's go out and find some girls and Jimi said 'No man let's just play' (or words to that effect) and apparently Jimi just walked around the flat with a guitar strapped on playing constantly! He turned out to be quite good(!), so there is something in this approach, which I take to be practice, practice, practice.

THINGS YOU <u>DON'T NEED</u> TO KNOW INITIALLY

This is going to be controversial, but in my opinion, when first starting to learn guitar you don't need to know or do the following:

To Learn Music Theory

Yes, it is beneficial, and certainly as you continue on your guitar playing journey it will be good to learn at least some theory, but it's not essential when you're starting out.

To Learn Every Note on the Finger Board

But again, it's very important to learn some. At the very least the first three frets of the 6th and 5th string (the Low E and the A) and preferably the 4th string too. This is only 9 notes, after all. From there it is helpful to learn the notes of the 6th and 5th strings all the way up to the 12th fret, so that when you are proficient at barre chords, you can rock out all the way along the neck.

To Learn Every Genre of Music

I can confidently predict that you have a favourite type of music and this is what you want to play. It will, of course, be natural to start learning this genre, however, over time trying other types of music will, in my view, make you a better player. As examples, Funk teaches you how to play great rhythm, for example including hammered on chords, Jazz can teach you new expanded chords that you might not encounter as often in other music, and Blues can teach you how to bring touch and feel to your playing, whilst Metal can teach you how to chug(!) and how to tame and work with distortion. So the lesson here, in my opinion, is that when you're ready, you should try playing other types of music, but you don't need to focus on this from the outset.

To Learn Scales and Modes

In all probability, you will be starting out playing open chords initially. This is indeed the best place to start in my view, as it will allow you to quickly begin playing songs. Think of all the songs that require just three chords, and once you can master four chords, well then there are a huge number of songs within your grasp. Did you know that The Beat Goes On by Sonny & Cher has only one chord throughout? An F in fact (or an open D played with a capo on the third fret). A pretty successful song it's fair to say, which shows that you don't need many chords to get going.

In my opinion, you don't need to focus on scales and modes right from the off. Once you have mastered a large number of chords, then it is worth learning the Major, Minor, Pentatonic and the Blues scale. The Blues Scale is the Pentatonic scale with the addition of a further note, so once you have one in the locker you have the other as well in double-quick time!

It is worth adding the Major scale to your arsenal as all other scales are derived from this, so learning this scale is massively helpful and something I wish I'd done many years ago! Learning these can be your introduction to playing lead and more specifically solos, but again you don't need to start with these unless you really want to - in which case go for it, but learn chords too!

To Practice Every Waking Hour

Don't misunderstand me - you definitely do need to practice. This is the only way that you will get better! It is not, however, necessary to set yourself the goal of doing a minimum of 3 hours practice a day and actually when you're starting out this is going to give you painful fingers and could put you off. I've heard that Steve Vai played for 7 hours every day when he was starting out, but I think initially it is better to do 30 minutes to an hour every day if possible and to practice correctly. Whatever practice regime you give yourself, make sure that it is often, but not so often as it becomes a chore and sucks the enjoyment out of the experience.

At the end of the day playing guitar should be enjoyable. So definitely end your practice doing something that you enjoy, be it playing a song you love or nailing a particular technique, as this will reinforce the enjoyment you get from your playing.

TUNING YOUR GUITAR

I strongly recommend that you invest in a guitar tuner. As I've already stated these can be very inexpensive and having your guitar in tune is <u>EXTREMELY</u> important!

It is however also worth knowing how to tune your guitar without a tuner, and I will explain how this can be done in a second, but first off you need a note that is in tune to start you off. People usually use A, so if you don't have a tuning fork (these are also very inexpensive by the way) a way to do this is to find a tune with A in it to be your reference guide. The first note of Stairway to Heaven, for example, is an A, actually played on the seventh fret of the D string rather than the open 5th string (but still usable) although you might find another tune that starts off with the open A, i.e. 5th string open.

Bear in mind when you are tuning that some strings might be flat and require tuning up and some might be sharp and require tuning down. Be careful when tuning up, because you might be taking the string higher than it wants to go and this will cause it to snap, and you don't want a snapped string catching your eye!

Once you have found your A note, let's imagine you are using Stairway to Heaven as your reference, then you need the 6th string the Low E to sound in unison, i.e. the same when fretted at the 5th fret. Hit the fretted note and work out if that sounds sharp or flat. If you're not sure, fret the string at the 6th fret and see if that makes it sound closer to the note your now aiming for, i.e. the A or further away. This will help tell you if you need to tune up or down. Once you think you have the notes matching play them together, i.e. pluck them at the same time. They should resonate at the same frequency and sound the same. It's less easy to see this if you play one after the other when you're less familiar with this technique.

Once you achieve this, then the 5th string, the A, needs to sound the same as the 6th string fretted at the 5th fret.

When that's done, fret the 5th string (the A string) at the 5th fret and get the 4th string (D) to sound in unison. We're halfway there!

Now fret the 4th string at the 5th fret and get the 3rd string to sound in unison.

Two strings to go! However, at this point we encounter a quirk of the guitar, which is that the 2nd string is tuned differently to the others. It's the odd one out, and just for this string, we need to fret the 3rd string or G at the fourth fret and get the 2nd string to sound in unison.

Final string, the high E or first string. Now we're back fretting at the fifth fret. Fret the 2nd string at the fifth fret and get the E string to sound in unison.

Job Done!

There are a few players who get around the fact that the 2nd or B string is usually tuned to a fourth, i.e. the fourth fret of the G string as shown above, by tuning it on the fifth fret, which tunes the B string to a C and tuning the first string off of the second string fretted at the fifth fret, which now makes the high E string tuned to F.

I'm not sure what the benefits of doing this are, however, it does means that all the standard chord shapes you might have spent weeks learning will no longer work and have to be altered. Given that most TAB is also written with standard tuning in mind this will not work either unless the player compensates by adding a fret higher on the second and first strings to whatever is shown on the TAB. So, all things considered, this is offered for interest only, and I would not recommend starting out with this tuning.

ALTERNATIVE TUNINGS

Eb (tuning all strings down a semi tone)

You might wonder what the point of doing this is, but it has two key advantages. It does alter the tone slightly, making it darker and heavier, but more importantly it takes some of the tension out of the strings making them easier to bend. This has led to this tuning being very popular and famous guitarist that have used it include Jimi Hendrix, Steve Ray Vaughan and Slash. I've also seen it argued that it makes Strats sound better, supposedly because of the length of the neck. This is clearly subjective though, but nevertheless I think there might be something to this, but without a doubt, it makes them slightly easier to play, because of the reduced string tension.

The good thing about this tuning is that all the usual chord shapes in standard tuning work in this tuning, so there's no need to learn new shapes. The only downside that I'm aware of with this tuning is that it is not popular with keyboard players, as it makes their job harder. So, if you have a keyboard player in the band, then they will probably not thank you for wanting to play in Eb.

Drop D (tuning the Low E string down to D)

This is a very popular tuning for Metal (listen to Avenged Sevenfold as a good example). This tuning is easy to achieve. It only involves re-tuning one string, although always check the others are these are put slightly out of tune as well by the reduced tension on the neck. This tuning has the advantage that it means you can play one-fingered power chords, and this, in turn, makes very fast chord changes possible.

DADGAD (tuning the Low E down to D, the B string down to A and Top E down to D)

This is commonly used in folk music, however you can also hear this on the track *Kashmir* by Led Zep. It gives the tune a big and different sound. However you do have to adopt different fingering to play chords, so this will be one to work on once you are proficient at reading TAB.

TIPS FOR BETTER PLAYING

Choose a guitar that's comfortable to use sitting down, because this is how you will spend most of your practice time, at least initially. This should steer you away from the pointy shaped guitars and Flying Vs, but it's your call at the end of the day!

Hold the guitar properly. Now some players adopt the 'classical guitar' pose with the guitar resting on their left leg and the neck sticking up at an angle of about 45 degrees, but it is more comfortable and natural to rest the guitar on your right leg (assuming you're right-handed). Bring the guitar into your body, so it's resting lightly against you. This should allow you to control the guitar – you don't want it flopping around! The neck should be roughly horizontal (actually it will be very slightly pointing upwards).

Put your thumb at the back of the guitar initially. When you're more proficient, you will be able to wrap your thumb over the top of the neck if you want or need to (doing this helps with some chords) but when you're starting out, it's best to avoid this.

Hold your pick correctly. It should be held between your thumb and first finger so that the tip comes out at a right angle to your thumb (it should not be pointing in the same direction as your thumbnail, if it is you'll need to cock your hand in an odd way to hit the strings – this is all wrong, so don't do that!).

Strum from the wrist. Keep your arm loose and let your wrist do the work, not your whole arm. Some people, when starting out, believe they need to strum by moving the whole of the arm from the elbow – this is not the case. Watch someone like Nile Rodgers of Chic, and you will see that the action is all in the wrist!

HAND PLACEMENT

In terms of hand placement and thumb position, when fretting notes you should play with your fingertips. Don't use the soft pad of your fingers. These never toughen up and make it very difficult to produce a clear note. Your fingers should therefore curve around the neck of the guitar to allow you to use your fingertips. This also helps you to clear the strings, so that all the strings you want to hear can ring out and you're not unintentionally muting other strings.

Place your thumb in roughly the centre of the back of the neck. You might want to wrap your thumb over the guitar neck when you have become reasonably proficient, but when starting out, it's best to work on having the thumb resting on the back of the neck.

Top Tip – Draw a dot using felt pen on each fingertip

This will allow you to check to see that this is placed correctly on the strings. If you can't see the dot, you've fretted properly. This way you'll be certain you are fretting the string well and are more likely to get a decent sound.

PALM MUTING

Learn how to do palm muting. This is critical for playing Rock and Metal and can even let you do a passable impression of an electric guitar using an acoustic. This technique helps you to bring dynamics to your playing as some notes or chords are muted, or softened, and when you don't mute, the notes or chords ring out in the usual way. It is common, therefore to intersperse this technique with the usual strumming or picking within a song.

USE YOUR PINKY!

Use your little finger (or your pinky if you're American). You use it in chords, so why not use it with single notes too? This will help to build up its strength and makes faster playing easier, as you don't need to shift position so often.

PLAY SONGS

Start playing songs as soon as you can and seek to make these as musical as possible. Copying the way the original artist delivered the song will help with this, and you can then provide your own interpretation if you wish. Not all songs are difficult, particularly if you use 'power chords' (these are chords consisting of just two notes, technically the root of the chord and the 5th note in the scale - I cover these later).

GET IN TIME

Use a metronome to ensure that your timing is on point. It will help massively with your rhythm playing, which in turn will help greatly if and when you start to play with other people. Using backing tracks or playing along to original recordings is another way of developing your timing.

USE THE ON/OFF METHOD

To try this, place your fingers on the fretboard, as if you are going to hold down a chord of your choice. At this point, however, do not press down firmly. The fingertips should only be resting on the strings. Now pick out the notes of the chord, but only engage the fingertips i.e. press down firmly when you get to the string that they are resting on. For example, let's say you're playing an open Em chord (see chords section). Play the 6 string, then when you get to the 5 string press down with the second finger and then when you get to the 4 string press down with the third finger. Then play the remaining open strings.

Now practice using just single notes. Place your fingers so that they are just resting on the 6 string starting on the 5th fret so that all four fingers have a fret to themselves (you should be using the 5th, 6th, 7th and 8th frets). Now press down with the little finger/pinky and play the note. Now release the finger, so it is just clear of the string and play the 7th fret where your third finger should be. Try to keep the other fingers relaxed. Then release the third finger and repeat for the 6th fret. Repeat for the 5th fret.

Then do the exercise again in the other direction, i.e. working up from the 5th fret all the time trying to only apply pressure with the finger that is required to play the note required at that time. To assist with this imagine filling up with energy when it is required (being turned On), and then the energy is turned off when it is no longer required (turned Off, hence On/Off Method).

EFFECTIVE PICKING

After picking a string, rest the pick on the next string down. This will mean that your hand isn't flapping around in space ahead of the next note. Of course, it's not possible to do this after the top E, as you've run out of strings, but as a means of controlling you're playing this is worth practicing.

PRACTICE DYNAMICS

This is all about mixing up the volume level and attack of your playing and including gaps and pauses in what you play, or put more simply, making what you play sound more musical. It's easy to get the hang of this by practicing a chord progression or scale or riff by playing it loud to start with and then doing it again, but playing it quietly (don't turn the volume of your guitar down, this is all about how firmly you're picking). Then play it again starting off quiet and then getting louder and then the other way round starting loud and becoming quieter. Have a go using single notes too.

LISTEN CAREFULLY

Learn to listen. It will make you play better, know when to play and what to play. Don't just focus on what you're playing, but think about how it fits with what others are playing (even if for now this is just a backing track). This is also about learning when it's good not to be playing at the same volume or even not playing at all, for example, if there is an organ solo or the band want just bass and drums for that section.

Listening includes being conscious of your tone - after all, you want the sound that you're making to be as good as it can be and appropriate to the song being played or the element of the song, so you might want to change the tone during the song ,for example if there is a bridge or a breakdown.

KEEP IT SIMPLE

Simplify and add space when it's appropriate (this is similar to the point above). Imagine that you're having a conversation - this is not a constant stream of words. You need to say something interesting and then pause, so that the listener can absorb what you've said. You might need to stress certain words to get your point across, or repeat things either in the same way or slightly re-phrased. Good musical expression is much the same as this, and ultimately you want it to come to some sort of conclusion, or resolve to use a bit of musical jargon, which probably means coming back to the root chord or note of the key you're playing in.

BE CREATIVE!

Sure, you will want to replicate the songs and sounds of the bands you love, but think also about how you can use what you know to create your own music.

DON'T BE DIRTY ALL THE TIME!

Use your Distortion or Overdrive, but probably not all the time. Play with a clean tone as well some of the time. There is a school of thought that says you should learn to play a piece of music clean first and then add the distortion later. I don't agree with this. Playing with distortion is an art in itself, and the only way to learn this is to use it, so you know how to get the best from it, and this includes being able to tame the distortion level when required. There are a variety of ways of achieving this, for example:

- through the use of palm muting

- by picking less aggressively

- by turning the volume of the guitar down (this can clean up the pickups)

LEARN THE WHOLE SONG!

You might find it satisfying to be able to reproduce the intro to one of your favourite songs, but if you're playing to other people they are going to expect to hear the whole song. You don't want them to go from 'Oh Wow!' to 'Oh Dear!'. This doesn't mean that you need to know the blistering solo as well (but if you do all the more kudos for you!). You should though know all the elements of the song bar that, which should include the chords that are played under the solo.

AIM TO NAIL IT!

Play everything as well as you possibly can. Try and nail whatever it is you're working on be it chords or riffs or scales or solos. This might mean playing it slowly to start with, maybe even very slowly. If you're struggling to get it down, then slow your playing down to the point where you can get it right (you should aim for 100% accuracy, not just being in the right ballpark) then speed up slowly until you have it at recorded speed or even faster! Playing slowly initially will allow you to concentrate on all aspects of what you're playing. Are you including all the right notes? Are the phrasing and dynamics correct?

Once you've built up the speed so that you can reproduce the tune at the recorded tempo you can take it even slightly beyond that, which might sound odd, but if you can play it slightly faster than the required speed then when you come to do this in front of your friends or an audience you should find it relatively easy.

UNDERSTAND BASIC MUSIC THEORY

Hang on you're thinking, didn't you say earlier that I don't need this? Well, yes, you don't need to go massively in-depth on this. It is after all possible to start learning guitar and playing songs very quickly by reference to chord boxes and TAB , which we'll come on to below, but understanding some music theory will greatly assist in your future exploration of the instrument. Some of the key things to know are: intervals (the gap between the notes), the major scale, pentatonic scale and blues scale in various positions.

If you wish to learn more about theory I can highly recommend:

Music Theory 101 by Boone and Schonbrun (published by Adams Media) as a very good introduction.

GREAT PLAYERS ARE THE RESULT OF PRACTICE

Remember that you're not born with talent; it takes practice! Once you've got your guitar, you need to put in the hours, including for the On/Off method covered above, which might take a bit of getting used to, but will aid you massively in the long run.

BAD HABITS TO AVOID

THE DEATH GRIP!

Try not to adopt a death grip! This is where you hold the neck of the guitar so fiercely that it is as if you're trying to throttle the life out of it. This is easier said than done when you're starting out, as you'll need to push down firmly with your fingers to get the notes to ring out and this will involve applying pressure with your grip. The ideal, however, is to only apply the pressure when you come to play the actual note – see the On/Off method above.

STOP NOODLING!

This is mindless playing if you're not familiar with the term, such as lead runs that lack any musical merit. Recognise it and stop as soon as you detect that you're doing it! Instead, take the idea you started with and find a chord shape, for example, tap out a tempo with your foot and put it into tune. This will also help with your creativity. Alternatively, learn tunes, as this will help provide a focus and stop you from straying into noodling territory.

ANCHORING

Don't anchor your hand on the bridge or body of the guitar. Let it float, as this gives you more dynamic control. This isn't a golden rule though, as there could be times when you want your hand near the strings for palm muting effects for example, but probably not all the time and for some techniques such as Funk style rhythm playing you can't achieve this with your hand welded to the bridge or body of the guitar. This is one to be conscious of and think whether it's appropriate to what you're playing at the time.

OVER-USE OF EFFECTS

Stop using so much reverb, or indeed any other effects that you start to use as a crutch. If you find they are covering up mistakes and shortcomings, turn them off for a while and try playing without them, so you can hear precisely what you're playing.

WORRYING ABOUT YOUR HANDS!

Thinking that your hands are too small or too big! Do not use this as an excuse. There is a famous player called Django Reinhart who lost two of his fingers in a fire, but he was an incredible player. Same goes for Tonni Iommi of Black Sabbath fame, who chopped a bit of one of his fingers off and has a metal replacement! So, the moral of the story here is work with what you have! It might not feel natural initially when you start to hold a guitar for the first time, because this is not a position we adopt in everyday life in anything else that I can think of. But, the more you do it, the more natural it will feel, until it becomes second nature.

11

What Are Guitar Chords?

As far as I'm concerned, it's no good

being able to wail out smokin' leads

if your rhythm chops suck!

Dimebag Darrell

Chords are any combination of 3 or more notes. They can be found on any instrument that can play at least 2 notes. In addition to the guitar, you see chords on bass, piano, banjo, and other string instruments. But singers and instruments like trumpets and saxophones can only play one note at a time, so they aren't able to produce chords.

There are 12 notes to choose from, and octaves typically aren't included in this number. So, if you're playing a G major chord on the 3rd fret of your E string, you're actually only playing 3 notes, and the other 3 strings are playing different octaves of those notes. It's possible to use any combination of 3 or more notes to produce a chord, but typically you choose notes from a scale.

WHAT ARE MAJOR CHORDS?

Major chords sound "happy" in tone and are often the first few chords that we learn. Most likely you will learn G, C, D, F, A and E Major pretty early on in your guitar playing journey, and that's because these are some of the most fundamental chords. Technically a Major chord is created by taking any note and adding the Major Third and the Perfect Fifth. So, in the earlier example of the G Major chord, this is made up of the notes G (the Root note), B (the Major Third), and D (the Perfect Fifth).

WHAT ARE MINOR CHORDS?

Minor chords are the "sad" version of a major chord. The only difference between a Major chord and a Minor chord is the third. Rather than a Major Third, they have a Minor Third, but both Major and Minor chords have a Perfect Fifth. Despite having only one different note, a Minor chord sounds very different from a Major one. The most common Minor guitar chords are Am, Em, and Dm and we'll cover how to play these below.

WHAT ARE CHORD BOXES?

These boxes show you where to put your fingers on the fingerboard to play chords. They consist of 6 vertical lines where each line represents a string. On these are placed numbers, where each number represents the finger that is usually used (there are times when you can choose to use different fingering, but when you're starting out it's a good idea to use the fingering suggested). Number 1 indicates your first finger, 2 your second finger, 3 your ring finger and 4 your little finger or pinky. You will sometimes also see T used to indicate the thumb where this is wrapped over the top of the fingerboard to fret a string usually the low E. In addition to these numbers you will see X and O used. X indicates that this string should not be played so it should not be picked or it should be muted by the use of other fingers or the right hand (for right-handed players). O is used to indicate that the string with the O on it should be played open, i.e. not fretted.

KEY CHORDS TO LEARN FIRST

This book is not about learning to play the guitar as such, it is about beginning your guitar adventure. There are many books on the market to assist you in learning the instrument, and as I've shown earlier on in this book also many free YouTube resources that you can draw upon. Nevertheless, given that learning how to play the guitar is as simple as mastering a few basic chords, it seems sensible to tell you which ones to start with. This section will, therefore introduce you to nine essential chords and show you how to play them properly (or more accurately in the usual or standard way). With practice, you'll soon be making music and then ready to progress to more complex chords, many of which build on these, for example by adding the fourth finger to play seventh chords (by adding the 7th note of the scale of the chord being played).

As explained above under Chord Boxes, the small numbers within the dots on the accompanying diagrams illustrate which fingers of your fretting hand you should use to play each note. The notes to the right-hand side show the fret number, so the 3 represents fret 3.

MAJOR OPEN CHORDS

Note that major chords are often referred to by omitting the major reference, so for example a G Major is referred to as a G and D major as a D and so on.

G Major (G)	
Play all the strings. 	As with most chords in this list, creating a clear sounding G Major chord depends on curling your first finger, so the open fourth string rings clearly. A variation to that shown is to not fret with your first finger as illustrated here but to mute the 5 string with your second by lightly allowing it to rest gently against the 5 string.

C Major (C)

Do not play the 6 string (Bottom E).

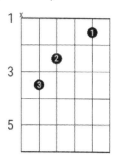

The C major chord is often one of the first chords guitarists learn. The fingering is fairly simple, although it may feel like a bit of a stretch initially. The key is to concentrate on curling your fingers, but in particular your first finger, so that the first open string rings out properly.

D Major (D)

Do not play the 6 or 5 strings (Bottom E and A).

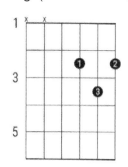

The D major chord is another extremely common beginner guitar chord. Remember to curl your third finger on the second string to stop you from muting the first string. It's important to only strum the top four strings, avoiding the open sixth and fifth strings. It is not a disaster if you hit the 5 string as there is an A note in the chord, but it will not sound good if you hit the 6 string which is an E note and is not in the chord. It is, however, best, for now, to concentrate on just hitting the final 4 strings.

135

A Major (A) Do not play the 6 string (Bottom E) 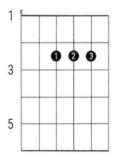	The A major chord can present a bit of a problem for new guitarists because all three fingers need to fit on the second fret on adjacent strings, which is a bit of a squeeze. Be sure the open first string is ringing clearly by curling your third finger. You can also find that the first finger is pushed quite far away from the fret, so you will need to press quite firmly with this finger to get a good sound.
F Major (F) **(Easy Shape)** Do not play the 6 or 5 strings (Bottom E and A). 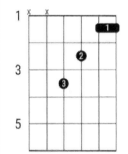	The F Major chord is one that requires us to shorten all the strings using a barre with the first finger. This chord box shows a simplified way of playing it, which is easier when you're starting out as you only need to barre the top two strings (the B and the top E). The full version of the chord involves using your first finger to barre, or fret, all the strings at the first fret and to place your third finger on the third fret of the 5 string and the fourth or pinky to fret the third fret of the 4 string, with the second finger on the second fret of the 3 string (as shown on the chord box). This requires a bit of practice to build up the strength in your first finger for this chord.

E Major (E)

Play all the strings.

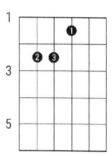

Another very common chord is the E major chord. Again, this is fairly straightforward to play. Make sure your first finger (holding down the first fret on the third string, the G) is properly curled or again the open second string, the B, won't ring out properly. Strum all six strings.

MINOR OPEN CHORDS

A minor (Am)

Do not play the 6 string (Bottom E).

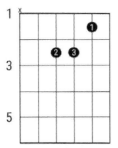

If you know how to play an E Major chord (see above), then you know how to play an A minor chord! All you need to do it move the whole chord shape down one string. Make sure your first finger is curled, so the open first string rings clearly. Avoid playing the open sixth string when strumming the A minor chord, as although it is a note in the chord you want to emphasis the A note in the bass.

E minor (Em)

Play all the strings.

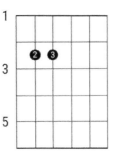

The E minor chord is one of the simplest to play, because you only use two fingers. Take extra care not to allow either of them to touch any of the open strings, or the chord won't ring out properly.

D minor (Dm)	The D minor is another fairly simple chord, yet many beginner guitarists find it tricky. Watch your third finger on the second string; if it isn't curled properly it will mute the first string. Be sure to only play the top four strings when strumming a D minor chord. It's not a disaster if you hit the open A string because this note is in the chord (fretted by your second finger) but its best to target the open D string as the first string you play.
Do not play the 6 or 5 strings (Bottom E and A). 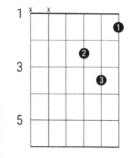	

CHANGING BETWEEN OPEN CHORDS

The key thing to remember here is that when changing from one chord to another move as few fingers as possible. Let's take changing from Am to C. In this case two of the fingers don't need to move (the first finger on the first fret of the B string and second finger on the second fret of the D string) so keep them where they are and just move the third finger to the new position (the third fret of the A string).

A further example would be moving from a D to a Dm. In this case, the third finger can stay where it is, and the other two fingers move position. In this example move the first finger from the second fret G string to the first fret top e string and the second finger from the second fret top e up two strings to the second fret G string.

Practice this concept, as it will help you to change chords more swiftly, as you pivot from a known point into the new chord. It also keeps your fingers closer to the finger board, which is a good thing.

BARRE CHORDS AND THE CAPO

So, from the above you have learnt about chords where some of the strings are not fretted at all hence the term 'open' chords, sometimes also referred to as Cowboy Chords, or so I'm told. These are extremely useful, but do restrict your playing to largely the first three frets of the guitar. This does mean that some chords can't easily be played. What to do? Well, the solution is the barre chord! What this does is essentially shorten the length of the guitar strings/fretboard by barring it with the first finger. This is the same effect as if you used a capo, this cunning device blocks off the strings at a fret of your choosing. This also has the effect of shortening the guitar strings, but once in place that is pretty much stuck there and is very hard to move mid-song (unless it's just hastily removed altogether in order to return to the normal string length).

Were a capo to be used, it would then allow you to use the open chords above, but they would then become different chords, so if for example the capo was on the second fret then playing a G major open chord as shown in the fret boxes above would be an A major chord. The capo, therefore, is a handy device should you want to sing a song, but find that it is a bit low for your voice with the chords as written. You can therefore use a capo to change the pitch to suit your voice by moving it up the neck until you find a pitch that's just right for you.

The capo does have its limitations though, the main one being that it will probably need to stay where you place it for the duration of the song and when placed at the desired fret you'll almost certainly need to tweak your tuning as the capo will pull some of the strings slightly out of tune. It is widely used in acoustic playing and folk music though because of the variety it allows you to have with very few chords (such as the ones shown earlier).

Still, for more flexibility, you need a different solution – enter the barre chord! As indicated above, this delivers the same effect, but with your first finger in the role of capo. This is extremely important for opening up all elements of the fingerboard and giving you access to new chords that are beyond open chords (even the F major chord shown above is straying into the barre chord territory and to play it in full it would be barred across all the strings of the first fret).

Typically, you play the major and minor shapes with your middle, ring and little finger/pinky. This then opens up the world of Rock and indeed Funk. By shifting the chord shape up and down the fretboard, you instantly get a new chord so, for example, an E major shape played by barring at the third fret is a G major chord (see the chord box above for the F major and imagine that the barre is covering all six strings not just the two shown in the chord box and that this barre is happening on the third fret). Shift this same chord up two frets more, and it becomes an A major. Take it up a further two frets and lift off the index finger and you have an E minor (Em) shape, but because it is barred at the 7th fret, it is now a B minor (Bm) chord. Given there are minimal changes required (you're for the most part just shifting the position of the same chord shape) this makes chord changes very speedy (once you've mastered the art) so extremely important in taking your playing to another level of proficiency.

POWER CHORDS

Now you're familiar with the concept let's make it even easier and Rockier! (Yes, I'm sure that is a proper word). We're going to take our newly learnt barre chords and just focus on the first two notes. Technically this is the first or root note and the fifth, so these power chords are denoted as the root plus a number 5, e.g. A5 (often played as the fifth fret of the low E string and the seventh fret of the A string). It is also possible to add the octave as well to make a slightly bigger sound, which would be achieved by also fretting the seventh fret of the D string in my A5 example. You'd now be playing three strings, but only two notes as the A note is just repeated.

Power chords have some distinct advantages when it comes to Rock and Metal. They are very fast to move - you only have two or perhaps three strings to worry about so there's less friction when sliding the chords to a new position and importantly, because they do not include the third (or minor third) can be played over either a Major or Minor chord (so you can let the keyboard guy or gal do that fiddly bit while you focus on the bass bit and the rhythm).

It's possible to take this to an even simpler place when using Drop D tuning as then all you need is to barre the Low E, and A strings and D string (if desired) but this a subject in its own right. For now, I would concentrate on playing in standard tuning (but the choice is yours!).

PALM MUTING

Once you have barre chords down, you can add these two techniques to add spice to your playing. The first of these, palm muting, is extremely important to rhythm playing. It's achieved by lightly resting the fleshy pad of your picking hand against the strings. Imagine you doing a Karate chop with your hand - it's the edge of your hand furthest from your thumb that I'm referring to here. The technique requires that you both have this part of your hand resting fairly lightly on the strings, whilst also strumming the strings. If your using power chords this doesn't require much movement by the pick. You can alter the amount of pressure you apply with the palm to the strings (too much and it will kill off the sound completely, which is not what you want, but not enough and you will not be able to hear the effect). As with most techniques on the guitar, this requires a bit of practice initially. However, it will eventually become instinctive and given it's so important for Rock and Metal it is something worth devoting time to mastering.

UPSTROKES

What about upstrokes? Well, these are a means of adding emphasis to the beat, for example. Have a listen to Green Onions by Booker T and the MGs for a great illustration of the impact that upstrokes can have. On this track, Steve Cropper plays short sharp upstrokes on the chords (I believe on the second beat of the bar), and this helps give the tune a driving sound. It's a great and relatively simple way of adding emphasis. It is, however, good if you can master not only the upstroke but also relaxing the pressure of your fretting hand after playing the upstroke as this makes it more staccato (as achieved on Green Onions).

12

What is TAB?

A lot of people think that if they learn to read music they are gonna lose their feel or their groove or something.

It's the stupidest thing I have ever heard.

Frank Gambale

TAB is a form of musical notation that was developed to set down guitar music and means that guitarists do not now need to be able to read stave (or the typical music you see with quavers and semi-quavers and all that). I heard it was developed so that people could set down what Eddie Van Halen was playing, this was recounted by him, and I've no idea if there is any truth in it. Nevertheless, regardless of how it came into being it is a fantastic innovation because it makes understanding what is played on a piece of music extremely easy, which is not to say that actually playing it will be, but at least we can see very clearly what the right notes are.

TAB is 6 horizontal lines, where each line represents the six strings of the guitar. The top line is for the top E (string 1), and the lowest line is for the bottom E (string 6).

Numbers are placed on each line to show the fret number that should be played. If there is no number on a string, then that means it shouldn't be played, and as with chord boxes, an O shows that the string should be played open. Sometimes the stave (original music notation) is also included. This isn't strictly necessary, however it does help to show how the music is moving, for example whether it's going up or down, or sideways for that matter and gives an indication of the duration of the notes.

This single bar of TAB below shows you how it can sometimes look.

109   12/8 Gtr I

```
|-5-----x-5--5--5---x--5--5-|----|
|-6-----x-6--6--6---x--6--6-|----|
|-5-----x-5--5--5---x--5--5-|----|
|-7-----x-7--7--7---x--7--7-|----|
|-5-----x-5--5--5---x--5--5-|----|
|.-------------------------|----|
```

The four bars of music below also show the tempo (the speed the music is intended to be played at) and how many beats there are to each bar. In this example it's in 4/4 time, which is the most common time signature.

This brief piece of music shows an ascending theme with single notes that then ends with an E chord in the final bar and you can see that all the strings are intended to be played or strummed together. There is also an example of a pull-off in the 3rd bar, which is indicated by the line joining the two notes, as the first note is higher than the second this shows that the first note should be pulled off the fretboard to sound out the second note (in this case the open D string).

Where the notes are stacked one above the other, this indicates that they should be played together. As a consequence, it's possible to represent chords on TAB instead of using Chord boxes, as shown by the final bar in this example.

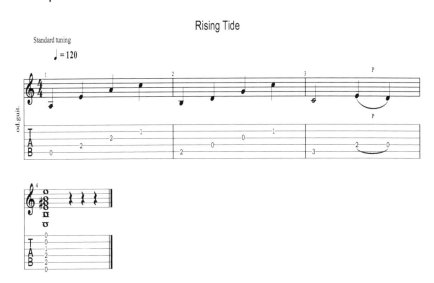

Rising Tide

In the example below, this is showing a Blues in E. This has a rolling bass, which is very common in Blues rhythm playing. This is where you add a note intermittently above the fifth of the scale, so taking the first bar the open Low E and the 2nd fret of the A string gives an E power chord. To this the 4th fret of the A is then played on the 2nd and 4th beats of the bar. The same pattern is repeated in the A and B positions before ending on E7#9 chords (the chord made famous, if indeed a chord can be made famous(?), by the track *Purple Haze*).

Rolling Bass Blues

13

Scales

Scales are the grammar of music.

Frances Parkinson Keyes

MAJOR AND PENTATONIC

Great, so we have covered the elements that you will need in order to become an awesome rhythm player, but let's say that you yearn to be a Rock God and everyone knows that this means mastering the art of the searing solo! How to work on this element? Well first off you need to know which notes are going to sound good together and this is achieved by learning scales. The best one to learn in this regard is the Major scale (most start with the Blues Pentatonic, but will get to that in a bit).

Why the Major scale? Well, it is the basis for all scales, so, for example, a Minor scale is the Major scale, but with a flat third note in the scale and the Major Pentatonic is the Major scale with some of the notes removed! Well worth learning then.

What about the Pentatonic scale? Well, this is worth learning because it is so widely used as the basis for Blues and Rock particularly the Minor Pentatonic and indeed often also in Metal as well. The basic (first position) shape for the Minor Pentatonic is straightforward to learn, and you can quickly sound pretty good by playing this over a Blues backing track. For example, if you want to play a Blues in A, you play the first position Minor Pentatonic shape at the fifth fret, i.e. starting on the A root note. This will get you playing the right notes. It is then about making it sound musical.

When learning scales, it's easy to fall into the trap of learning a 'box' shape. This is the notes of the scale working your way down the fretboard vertically from the bottom E (6 string) to the top e (1 string). This can mask what is actually happening with the scale and fixes a shape and finger positions in your mind rather learning the intervals (or gaps) between the notes.

As a result, it is initially a good idea to also learn the scales along one string. This might seem rather basic, but it has the merit of allowing you to grasp the make-up of the scale more quickly. Added to which by shifting the root note you can immediately play a new scale by following the pattern. Let's take a look at what these patterns are.

THE MAJOR SCALE

This has the following structure.

Note 1) The Root

Note 2) is a Whole Step up from the root (note 1)

Note 3) is a Whole Step up from note 2

Note 4) is a Half step up from note 3

Note 5) is a Whole step up from note 4

Note 6) is a Whole step up from note 5

Note 7) is a Whole step up from note 6

Note 8) is a Half step up from note 7, which takes us back to the root note.

To express this more simply the 'formula' of intervals for a Major Scale is:

Whole, Whole, Half, Whole, Whole, Whole, Half

To practice this, start, say, on the G string second fret (an A note) and play an A Major scale by moving up the G string to the intervals shown above. As we have started on an A note, this is our root note, and the scale is an A Major scale. If you shift the first note up two frets onto the B and follow the same intervals as above, it transforms into a B Major scale and so on and so forth. Have a play with this moving your starting point to create new major scales with ease!

Once you have a grip on the sound of the major scale you can learn the following shape, which in this case is a G Major scale as the root note is a G (denoted by the R). You would probably therefore want to start this scale on the third fret of the E string and work your way down the scale and back up again if you wish, but you could also start on the second root note on the D string and go either up or down to start with. Remember to end your practice on the root note.

THE MAJOR SCALE

This neck diagram also shows the notes of the scale in terms of their position in the scale e.g. the 2 indicates it is the second and 3 that it is the third and so on.

G Major Scale

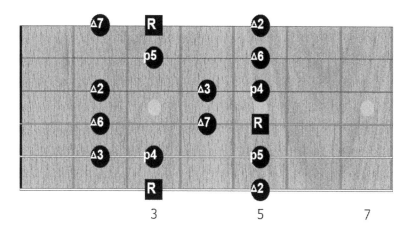

THE MAJOR PENTATONIC

In this scale we have dispensed with the 4th and the 7th notes when compared to the full major scale (as shown above). This makes it slightly easier to learn as you only have two notes per string across the whole scale.

G Major Pentatonic

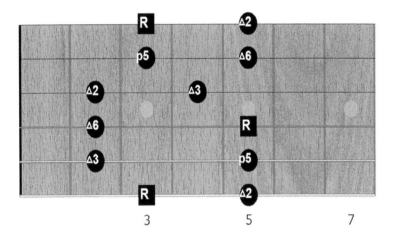

3   5   7

THE MINOR SCALE

Let's follow the same process to learn the Minor scale. Firstly, the intervals for the notes are as set out below. I suggest starting on the second fret G string again, because then you can see immediately the difference between the Major scale (learnt above and this one, the Minor scale).

Note 1 The Root

Note 2) is a Whole Step up from the root (note 1)

Note 3) is a Half Step up from note 2

Note 4) is a Whole step up from note 3

Note 5) is a Whole step up from note 4

Note 6) is a Half step up from note 5

Note 7) is Whole step up from note 6

Note 8) is a Whole step up from note 7, which takes us back to the root note.

To express this more simply the 'formula' of intervals for a Minor Scale is:

Whole, Half, Whole, Whole, Half, Whole, Whole

As with the Major scale changing the root note and following the intervals will give you a different minor scale. For the sake of variety, let's move to the fourth fret D string and make this our root note. Then using the intervals above we're now playing F# Minor.

Once you have a grip on the sound of the Minor scale you can learn the following shape, which in this case is a G Minor scale as the root note is a G (denoted by the R). Again, you can start your practice on any root note, but remember to also end on a root note.

G Minor Scale

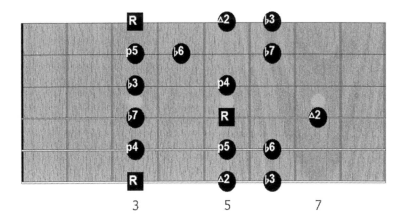

It's really worth embedding these scale ideas thoroughly. Once you've done this you can look at learning the standard scale boxes, then the same scales using 3 notes per string, this entails some stretching for some of the notes, or even 4 notes per string, which entails both stretching and sliding up. The latter two options are favoured by metal players and those that want to play quickly as they allow you to play legato and hammer-ons and pull-offs with relative ease.

Top Tip – Always return to the root

When learning scale shapes always play them so that you return to the root note. Often a scale shape will take you beyond the root note because there are other frets available and the scale shape will therefore show the second and third notes after the root for example. By all means, play these as well (they are part of the scale after all) but then play back down the notes of the scale until you return to the root note. This makes it sound better for a start, but also helps to reinforce where the root notes are.

THE MINOR PENTATONIC SCALE

This is often the first scale players learn (myself included). As the name suggests, it has five notes and removes the second and sixth notes from the minor scale. The beauty of this scale is it is easy to learn as the pattern in the first position has the first note of every string starting on the same fret. So, if we think of G pentatonic, for example, the root note is on the third fret of the bottom E (string 6) and when we move to another string these also all start on the third fret, so you just need to learn the second note on every string, which isn't too taxing!

This scale is extremely common is a wide variety of music so well worth learning and indeed some players have made a whole career out of pretty much just this scale (albeit in every position i.e. covering the whole neck).

G Minor Pentatonic Scale

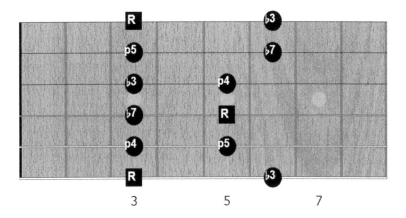

THE MINOR BLUES SCALE

Now we have a further variation on the theme, namely a hexatonic scale i.e. one with 6 notes. I've stuck with G, so that you can compare and contrast with the scale shape above. Close observation will show that this scale includes all the same notes as the pentatonic with the addition of the flat 5, which on this position (position 1) crops up on the A and G strings.

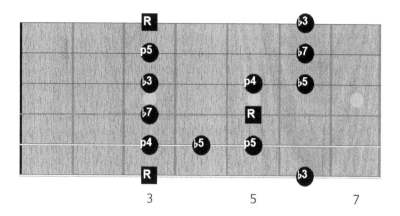

USING WHAT YOU KNOW

All very interesting, but how can I use these scales? Well once you're familiar with at least one of the shapes you can find a backing track on YouTube (there are loads available). So, for example let's say that you have learnt the G Blues Scale above. Type in Slow Blues in G and choose one you like the sound of. The backing track will probably be a 12 bar Blues (as the name suggests 12 bars are played through and then they repeat). In a G 12 bar Blues this will feature the chords G, C and D (possibly played as G7, C7 and D7 or even Gm, Cm, and Dm). Work on hitting sequences of notes that land on the relevant chord being played at that point i.e.

when the G is playing return to the root note above (which is the G) and when the C is playing play sequences with C in them that probably end on that note and the same for the D. This might take a bit of practice but will make your solos sound melodic and interesting. Once you have got to grips with this it's then just a case of expanding your understanding of the scale by learning the other positions so that you can cover the whole of the fret board.

14

Technique

(or - How to Sound Really Good!)

I don't deal in technique.

I deal in emotions.

Jimmy Page

You could, for example, throw in some of your palm muting perhaps, as this will make your playing sound more interesting if you use it sparingly to add a bit of spice, but what else...

GIVING IT FEEL!

There are other techniques that you can use to give your solo playing greater interest. These include:

SLIDES

Probably the easiest of the techniques, but not used as often as it warrants in my opinion. It entails literally fretting one note and sliding up or down to another note. There is a great example of this in the solo from Time by Pink Floyd (Dark Side of the Moon) where David Gilmour uses several slides, both up and down, towards the end of the solo. True he has some effects added as well, but this section using slides does change the vibe of the solo and fits very well with the more open feel of the tune at that stage.

BENDS

Extremely common and critical in getting your solos to sounds more interesting. These are typically where a note is fretted, and then you use the strength in your finger to bend the string upwards (although note that bends on the D and A strings are typically pulled downwards and the Low E is always pulled downwards as in this case that's the only option). This is often to take the fretted note up a whole step, i.e. a Whole tone. Sometimes it can be one and a half steps or at its most extreme even two whole steps (this takes some doing and light gauge strings!). David Gilmour is again a very proficient exponent of this technique. It can also be more subtle, with bends up only a half step (a Semitone) or even just a quarter-tone, often used in Blues to give just a bit of interest.

In addition to bends upwards, you can also bend the note up before you hit it and then release it back down to the original fretted note. This requires a bit of practice, as you need to know how far up to bend the note before you have actually sounded it, otherwise bend up not enough and it will be flat or too much, and it will be sharp.

Bending sharp or flat is something you need to avoid, or it can sound like a cat is being strangled and you don't want that. The way to test this when your practicing is to play the target note, say two frets up from the note you're going to play. Then play the bend – does it sound like the target note? Keep working on this until you can nail it most of the time. I'd start with the whole bend as this is very useful.

Once you have this technique in the locker, you could also add unison bends. These are where you play two notes at the same time, with one being bent up to the other note so that they ring out together. For example, fretting the fifth fret of the B string and the seventh fret of the G string and then hitting both these notes and very quickly after they start ringing out bend the G string up by a whole tone. It should then be the same pitch as the fretted B string. Listen to the end of *Stairway to Heaven* where Jimmy Page plays a series of ascending unison bends to end the song.

HAMMER ONS

These are where one note is fretted, and a higher note on the same string is fretted by hammering on the finger for the higher note. A good example would be to play the third fret of the G string with your first finger and then use the third finger to hammer onto the fifth fret. Typically, you pick the first note and let the second note ring out from the hammer on. This requires a bit of force from the finger doing the hammering on; otherwise, it won't sound out clearly.

PULL OFFS

More or less the reverse of the above. In this instance, we pick the first fretted note and then release the fretting finger to reveal a fretted note behind it. Let's say for example it is the fifth fret of the G which we're fretting with our third finger and then at the same time we are also fretting the third fret of the same string. We hit the first note (the fifth fret of the G string) and then lift the third finger so that the third fret note rings out. This requires us to slightly pull the string with the finger doing the pull off, you don't want to pull down too much though or it will pull the note out of tune. It does take a bit more practice therefore than the Hammer-Ons. Still, the two essentially go together and once mastered, will make a big difference in how your solo playing sounds, particularly when married with bends.

LEGATO

This is picking once, but then playing many notes! This is beloved of Metal players as it can significantly add speed, so if you want to shred this is one to work on. For example, let's take three notes per string, we're going to play the third fret of the Low E by picking it and then hammer on the fifth fret with our second finger (this is a big stretch) then the seventh fret with our little finger or pinky (another big stretch). You can then move this down a string and play the same frets of the A string (playing these two strings is actually the beginning of a G major scale and is how Metal players would play it as a means of playing quickly, so if Metal is your thing then worth learning how to play scales with 3 or even 4 notes per string and playing legato).

TAPPING

Think Eddie Van Halen's solo to Beat It! It's where you play notes by literally tapping the fingerboard with one or more fingers. This can create both great speed and depending on the notes played a wide interval (tonal gap) between the notes, so for example you can hit the open High E at the eighth fret, so that it rings out, and then hammer down on the fifth fret with one of the fingers of your fretting hand (I suggest either your first or middle finger) and then hit, or tap, the eighth fret with the tip of the first or second finger of your picking hand to get the note of that fret to ring out. I suggest considering the second finger because then you can continue to hold a pick between your thumb and first finger. Try doing this and repeating the sequence focusing on trying to slightly pluck the tapped note when you release your finger. This helps to make the notes ring out. You could then play the sequence through once and then on the second pass move the fretted notes down a fret (so you hammer onto the fourth fret and tap the seventh fret). You'll be tapping with the best of them in no time!

ALTERNATE PICKING

This is where you pick the notes with a down pick followed by an up pick. This is a means of playing faster. Most, if not all solos, use this technique. It is not necessarily apparent from the sound of the notes being played, this is more about getting around the fretboard with greater efficiency.

TREMOLO PICKING

This is alternate picking – but faster! The best example that I can think of for this is the opening to *Wasted Years* by Iron Maiden. It is where you pick the strings down and up very quickly. In the case of the *Wasted Years* intro this is all on the High E string. In this case the technique does alter the sound in my opinion.

15

Where to Turn for

Inspiration

Music is a moral law. It gives a soul to the Universe, wings to the mind, flight to the imagination, a charm to sadness, gaiety and life to everything.

It is the essence of order and leads to all that is good and just and beautiful.

Plato (no less!)

PLAYERS TO CHECK OUT

All guitarists find that they are influenced by players that have gone before them. This could be the original Blues players such as Robert Johnson or more recent guitarists from the sixties, seventies or eighties or those more recently. They can all potentially influence what you play and how you play it. You can use this in turn to create your own sound. Here are some players worth listening to and why. Bear in mind this is just my opinion. Clearly, this area is highly subjective, so this list might not be to everyone's taste.

You'll find that many of these guitarists favoured either Gibson Les Pauls or Fender Stratocasters, but that doesn't mean that you have to do so as well. You might latch onto a different guitar that is just right for you and produces 'your sound'.

BLUES INSPIRED GUITARISTS

Many of the guitarists that came to prominence during the sixties were heavily influenced by the earlier Blues guitarists such as Robert Johnson, BB King and Freddie King. Eric Clapton, for example, would go on to cover a number of the older Blues tracks including Crossroads with Cream, a track originally recorded by Robert Johnson back in the twenties and one of the very few tracks that he recorded before his death, having allegedly sold his soul to the devil!

Chuck Berry (18/10/1926 – 18/3/2017)

A massive influence on other musicians in his own right, for example, The Stones, Clapton and Hendrix, Led Zeppelin to name just a few, but his music drew heavily on the Blues. He was also a great showman and was very adept at producing catchy guitar intros for his songs such as the one on Johnny B Goode, which incidentally was named by Rolling Stone Magazine as the number one guitar song of all time!

In the 1970s he toured extensively playing his back catalogue and carried only his Gibson guitar (a Gibson ES-335) because he worked on the basis that he could hire a band that knew his tunes regardless of where he went! Early in his career, Bruce Springsteen was for a while one of the band members. He recounted that Berry didn't produce a set list or tell the band what he was about to play expecting them to work it out from the intro. As a guitarist, he was not a virtuoso when compared to others. Still, he did produce very distinctive music, which has stood the test of time. One of his tunes even features in the film Pulp Fiction.

Eric Clapton (30/3/1945 -)

As mentioned, Eric was heavily influenced by the earlier blues, and indeed the riff to Layla was an old blues riff that Eric sped up and the rest is history! His live album Just One Night is a good example of how important the blues is to him, and you can hear this in his playing through the use of the pentatonic scale and in his bends. He was ranked as second in the Rolling Stone list of the '100 Greatest Guitarists of All Time' and has sold more than 100 million records worldwide making him one of the best-selling musicians of all time. The highlights of his career to date were the huge success he had with the band Cream, Derek and the Dominos (with whom he recorded *Layla*) and a long solo career, which has included several standout hits including *Wonderful Tonight* and *Tears in*

Heaven. I personally like his work on the Roger Waters' album The Pros and Cons of Hitchhiking, in particular, the solo to *Sexual Revolution*, which I heard Roger Waters (of Pink Floyd-fame) state in an interview was done in one take(!), and it certainly sounds like it to me, as well as the music he contributed to 1985 BBC thriller Edge of Darkness, which is very emotive.

Eric is credited with the so-called "woman tone" from the Cream era, which he achieved using the neck pickup of a solid body guitar with humbuckers (usually his Gibson SG) with the tone control rolled all the way off and the volume control all the way up.

Peter Green (29/10/1946 – 25/7/2020)

Another guitarist who has been heavily influenced by the blues and played a significant role in the blues revival in the UK through his work with the early Fleetwood Mac band, which he founded. He began playing professionally at the age of 15, whilst also working. He recorded the song *Black Magic Women* (later covered by Santana) and the instrumental *Albatross*. He was renowned for string bending, vibrato and an economy of style such as on *Need Your Love So Bad*, when with Fleetwood Mac. He is well known for deriving a unique tone from his 1959 Les Paul, which was the result of it being wired 'incorrectly' so that the pickups were out of phase. He bought the guitar for £114 from Selmars in Charing Cross Road, which I believe was a bargain even then. The guitar was subsequently bought by Gary Moore and more recently Kirk Hammett of Metallica, who reputedly paid nearly $1m for it!

Alvin Lee (19/12/1944 - 6/3/2013)

Famed for his blisteringly fast solo playing before this was widely adopted. He made his name with Ten Years After who came to prominence as the result of their performance at Woodstock on Sunday 17 August 1969. He played a Gibson ES-335 nicknamed the 'Big Red' which he'd purchased for the princely sum of £45 in a Nottingham music store (including a case!).

Rory Gallagher (2/3/1948 – 14/6/1995)

He mixed the blues with a touch of traditional Irish music that made his playing very distinctive. His first album with his band Taste featured a number of supercharged blues numbers such as *Leaving Blues* and *Sugar Mama*. He played a well-worn sunburst 1961 Fender Stratocaster and was renowned for his live performances. He also used a Dallas Rangemaster Treble Booster in between his guitar and amp. He would later tell Brian May of Queen this fact, which in turn led to the Brian May tone when paired with Vox AC30 amps that we are familiar with on the later Queen albums (interestingly May's tone on earlier records is much more akin to that of Jimmy Page and Led Zep, so the treble booster was clearly a tone-defining addition).

Jimmy Page (6/1/1944 -)

Rolling Stone Magazine ranked Page as number 3 in their '100 Greatest Guitarists of All Time' list, and there is no doubt that he has been massively influential and is the master of the riff! Most famous as I'm sure you already know for his work with Led Zeppelin, but before that he was making a name for himself as a session musician even at one point playing the guitar solo on the 1965 Tom Jones hit *It's Not Unusual*! Page is on record as saying that at one point he was playing at least three sessions a day, six days a week. He then moved on to joining The Yardbirds (which might have come as a relief after all that session work!).

There are many great riffs that he produced whilst with Led Zep, such as *Whole Lotta Love* and *Heartbreaker*. He is equally at home playing acoustic as well as electric and uses a variety of different tunings. He was also famous for using a cello bow to create a droning noise from his electric guitars. Led Zep are one of the best-selling music groups in the history of recording, with estimates suggesting that their worldwide sales exceed 200 million albums. Page described his approach with Led Zep as wanting it to be:

'a marriage of blues, hard rock and acoustic music topped with heavy choruses – a combination that had never been done before. Lots of light and shade in the music.'

I'd say he succeeded.

Gary Moore (4/4/1952 – 6/2/2011)

Although left-handed Moore learned to play right-handed and went on to join the blues-rock band Skid Row (not to be confused with the American band of the same name) which also included Phil Lynott. Lynott went on to form Thin Lizzy and got Moore to join after the departure of Eric Bell. Moore's blues influence can clearly be heard on his work with Thin Lizzy (such as Black Rose). Subsequently, it was his primary focus for example on the album 1990 album Still Got The Blues which would go on to sell over 3 million copies worldwide. He cited his friend and mentor Peter Green as a major influence on is playing. Whilst apparently the best piece of advice he thought he ever received came from bluesman Albert King, who taught him the value of leaving space in his playing.

Stevie Ray Vaughan (3/10/1954 – 27/8/1990)

Firmly rooted in the blues and specifically Texas Blues. He became a Blues legend before his untimely death in a helicopter crash near East Troy, Wisconsin at the age of 35. He played in Eb with very heavy gauge strings and is worth listening to for his dynamics and tone. I especially like his awesome rendition of the Jimi Hendrix track *Little Wing*, a track which suited the tone of his Fender Stratocaster.

In fact, he cited Jimi as one of his greatest influences, saying:

"I love Hendrix for so many reasons. He was so much more than just a blues guitarist – he played damn well any kind of guitar he wanted. In fact, I'm not sure if he even played the guitar – he played music."

Paul Kossoff (14/9/1950 – 19/3/1976)

Another guitarist to die before his time at the tender age of 25. Paul Kossoff was the guitarist in the band Free and probably best known for the song *All Right Now*, which was a massive hit for them. He had joined the band when only 18 and Andy Fraser the bass player was only 16! Paul had seen John Mayall's Bluesbreakers playing live with Eric Clapton and soon purchased a vintage Gibson Les Paul as a result, and this was to be his trademark guitar. He coaxed huge sounds out of it as he paired it with a Fender bass amp.

Slash (23/7/1965 -)

Famous for his work with Guns N' Roses during the 1980s during which time he definitely gained Rock God status (it's worth noting that when he decided to devote himself to learning guitar, he practiced for up to 12 hours a day!). His solos are largely blues-based and very melodic (listen to *November Rain* for example, which Guitar World ranked as number 6 on their list of 'The 100 Greatest Guitar Solos' in 2008). He is most associated with playing Gibson Les Pauls, which he played tuned down a semitone to Eb. He has numerous signature guitars made by both Gibson and Epiphone. On stage, he uses Marshall amps, particularly the Silver Jubilee JCM 2555 amp. However, the famous album Appetite for Destruction was recorded using a rented Marshall 1959.

Angus Young (31/3/1955 -)

The schoolboy dressed Gibson SG-toting lead guitarist with AC/DC was, along with his Rhythm guitar-playing brother Malcolm, a tour de force. Their brand of heavy rock originated in the clubs of Australia where they had to have their Marshall amps cranked up loud. The band's music is significantly more complex than many give it credit for, sometimes wrongly assuming that is three chords and not much else. Angus always managed to weave a suitable solo into the band's tracks with the album Back in Black being a standout for me. The tracks often also drew on the Chuck Berry idea of an intro and more or less every song on Back on Black has a great intro in my view.

In terms of tone, Angus doesn't use as much distortion as some people might think, and his tone has pronounced bass range. He uses a combination of Gibson SGs through four 1959 Super Lead Plexi Reissue 100-watt heads with each head powering two 4x12 cabinets – now that's a wall of sound! In addition, he uses a 60s Marshall JTM45 (usually hidden under the stage) which I read he kicks in for his solos.

David Gilmour (6/3/1946 -)

One of my favourite guitar players and whilst he doesn't personally place much emphasis on Blues as a factor in his playing (interestingly saying it was just as much influenced by Folk music) I think his playing has significant Blues overtones from his choice of notes to his bends and slides. Famed for searing guitar solos, such as those with Pink Floyd on *Time* and *Comfortably Numb* he is also the master of dynamics, such as on *Shine on You Crazy Diamond* a track that developed out of the famous 4 note riff at its heart. He typically favoured Fender guitars – both Telecasters and Stratocasters. His famous 'Black Strat' became one of the most expensive guitars ever sold when it sold at a charity auction for US$3,975,000. If only I'd known it was coming up for auction (and was a billionaire!).

Mark Knopfler (12/8/1949 -)

I would struggle to say if Mark Knopfler or David Gilmour is my ultimate favourite guitarist, both have similar qualities in having wonderful dynamics and musicality in their playing. In Mark's case, he also developed an unorthodox playing style with the fingers on his picking hand that is very much unique to him and helps give him his specific sound, however, he does also play with a pick on occasion. His playing style was a development of his interest in Blues and Folk music. He says:

"I got involved in Folk music because I couldn't afford an amp."

Probably the clearest example of this is on the massive Dire Straits hit *Romeo and Juliet*, but more recently also the track *Postcards from Paraguay*. As far as his electric guitar playing is concerned, this probably reached its pinnacle with *Brothers in Arms* and *Telegraph Road*. Like David Gilmour, he began playing Fender Strats, although has subsequently played a variety of other guitars including a 1988 Pensa-Suhr Custom, which was one of his main guitars in the late 1980s and early 1990s. Like Gary Moore, he is left-handed, but learnt to play right-handed. It's not however just his virtuoso guitar playing that I'd admire, but the storytelling he achieves with his songs, which I think is first class.

Brian May (19/7/1947 -)

Co-founder of the band Queen with lead singer Freddie Mercury and drummer Roger Taylor, they would go on to become one of the biggest rock bands in the world following the release of *Bohemian Rhapsody* from the album A Night at the Opera. They were aided by May's virtuoso playing, which featured his own distinctive sound (but see reference to Rory Gallagher above) and multi-layered guitar work. Famously he largely uses his homemade guitar the Red Special, which was largely made from bits and pieces that he and is his father had to hand, including a tabletop for the body and an old mahogany mantelpiece for the neck and featured pickups he made himself. He also unusually uses old sixpence coins as picks and these no doubt also contribute to his tone and playing style. He typically pairs his guitar with Vox AC 30 amps.

Jimi Hendrix (27/11/1942 – 18/9/1970)

No list of players to listen to would be complete without the inclusion of Hendrix in my opinion, a player who was not only a virtuoso, but also significantly ahead of his time. He managed to combine complex rhythm playing with searing solos. He filled his sound out with the use of hammer-ons and pull-offs, which was important given that when he played with The Jimi Hendrix Experience, he was part of a three-piece band. This meant he needed to carry the main focus of the song and indeed he was adept at using the guitar as an electronic sound source, using things such as feedback, for example, in a controlled way to enhance his music. Rolling Stone ranked him as the greatest guitarist of all time. He died accidentally of asphyxia at the age of just 27, and we can only wonder what music he might have gone on to produce.

It's probably the case that his tone was generated as much from his fingers as from his equipment. Incidentally, he had very long fingers, which made his guitar necks seem very small and made it easy for him to play notes and chords that would be more of a stretch for those of us with shorter digits!

He was also an exponent of playing with his thumb over the top of the guitar neck, which also freed up his fingers to do more intricate fills, which he used to great effect in his rhythm playing. He was able to combine this playing with his solos, which worked so well in the context of the power-trio band he is mostly associated with. Listen in particular to his standout track *Little Wing*.

He came to play Fender Strats routinely and in particular ones with maple necks. He used Marshall 1959 Super Lead 100-Watt heads into Marshall 4x12 cabinets. In terms of effects he used Vox Wah, custom-made Roger Mayer Octavia, Dallas-Arbiter Fuzz Face and Univox Uni-Vibe, all plugged straight into the front of the amp.

Conclusion

So, in this book we've talked you through the key aspects of guitars both acoustic and electric and the features that impact on tone, such as the woods used in the body and neck, the hardware and of course the pickups in the case of electric guitars play a significant part in the tone. We even covered the number of strings available to you these days (if you're just starting out, I'd stick to 6). We've covered the type of budget you can expect to pay and what you'll get for your money as well as both where to buy and how to haggle! We've talked about amps and their key features. I advised you to get your guitar professionally set up. This is particularly important for electric guitars and especially those with tremolos fitted where the intonation can go out more easily.

If you're buying an electric guitar and you have got your amp purchase also sorted, then the chances are you are going to want to play with tone by buying some pedals, so we also covered the main ones and their uses.

Once your equipment is all in order you will want to learn to use it to maximum effect and we covered where to go for tuition and some of the YouTube channels to consider as resources as well as some on-line learning aids for consideration. We also looked at what to cover when you're first starting out – how to read chord charts and how to play basic open chords and explained what barre chords are. Then we looked at TAB the guitar notation that will unlock the whole neck for you! We then looked at some common scales (the grammar of the guitar). We then looked at the techniques, such as bends and hammer-ons and pull-offs that will make your playing sound more musical. Finally, we took a look at some players to listen to and why they have influenced others.

I hope you'll agree that we've covered a lot of ground, which will hopefully make your guitar journey not only better informed but more enjoyable as well.

Lastly, I want to leave you with a thought on how to approach your practice. Naturally learning the guitar is a motor skill and requires learning the techniques through repetition. This might feel slow at first but persevere! Once you start to string some of your learning together this will hopefully motivate you to continue with the guitar for many years to come.

To help with this it's worth considering the role that mind set plays on your success as a guitarist and musician. Top athletes and sportsmen and women, for example, have long understood that a key to their success lies in their mind set. The same is true for successful guitar players, regardless of whether they appreciate this point consciously or not. Here are the things to pay attention to:

Be Self-motivated!

It's most effective if the reason you're picking up the guitar is driven by you and not someone else nagging you! Make music because you want to not because of someone else's expectation.

Stay Positive, but also Realistic

Naturally you will want to improve your playing whether that is clearly playing every note of an open chord or more advanced techniques like sweep picking or legato, but be both positive in your mind set, have the attitude that you can improve your playing, but at the same time look for incremental (small steps) in this improvement. It is going to be disheartening if you're picking up the guitar for the first time with the thought that you can now set about nailing the second solo to *Comfortably Numb*. If you put the building blocks in place one day you can; but build up to it!

Be Focused

Practicing can take time and patience and if you are able to draw on long periods of concentration then you are most likely to succeed. If you are able to 'get in the zone' then you are more likely to perform well whether that's playing to a mate or up on stage playing to lots of people.

Develop Your Self-confidence

Part of this comes from putting in the work so that you know you can play what you want to play, but also remain positive and don't allow others to put you off you goal through their negativity (they may even be jealous of you for learning a skill that they don't have the motivation to do themselves).

Take Responsibility for Your Own Actions

Try not to make excuses for what hasn't gone well focus on the positive and see what you can do to fix it. Perhaps you need to work on a particular part of the song for example. Sometimes this might only be a single tricky bar – perhaps a chord change for example that you are finding difficult. Accept that this is the case and focus on it to improve it. This doesn't necessarily mean that you have to be able to nail it immediately but keep working on it over a few practice sessions and you will soon find that what was initially frustratingly hard has become playable and after a while as you keep working on it, you'll find it easy – trust me on this.

Well, we're at the end now. I've given you the tools you need to begin your guitar playing journey, in fact hopefully you have already begun this. Go out there and use what you now know.

Enjoy the ride!

If you enjoyed this book and got value from it, please leave a review on Amazon, as that would really help me and hopefully future readers too.

I'm signing off – it's time to Rock!

As Frank Zappa said – *Shut Up 'n Play Yer Guitar*.

All the best.

Steve Cabain

Author Profile

Steve Cabain has played guitar for over 40 years. He's been the lead guitarist in numerous bands and taken part in a number of recording sessions. He enjoys playing both acoustic and electric guitar and a variety of music styles, from Folk to Blues, through to Classic Rock and Metal.

He teaches guitar on a part-time basis and enjoys passing on his knowledge to others. He lives in Surrey, on the outskirts of London, and is married with three children and has an extensive guitar collection!

See **www.SteveCabain.com** for further info and post your thoughts on our Crucial Guitar Forum.

Please Review This Book!

If you enjoyed this book and got value from it, please leave a review on Amazon, as that would really help me and hopefully future readers too. Even critical points help me to refine the book even further and I read and am grateful for every review I receive.

The QR code below will take you straight to the review page.

Many Thanks! Steve

Printed in Great Britain
by Amazon